PENAN

Voice for the Borneo Rainforest

DR. WADE DAVIS
and
THOM HENLEY

Foreword by
DR. DAVID SUZUKI

Western Canada Wilderness Committee — WILD Campaign

DEDICATION

*To the Sarawak rainforest
and its native peoples—
so both will have
"a way to stay."*

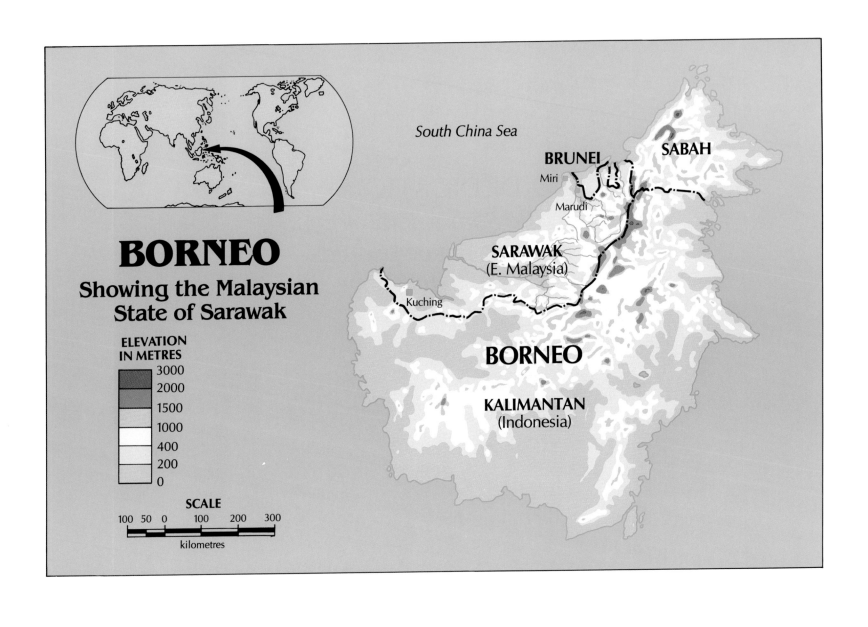

BORNEO

Showing the Malaysian State of Sarawak

ELEVATION IN METRES

3000
2000
1500
1000
400
200
0

SCALE

100 50 0 100 200 300

kilometres

South China Sea

BRUNEI

SABAH

Miri

Marudi

SARAWAK
(E. Malaysia)

Kuching

BORNEO

KALIMANTAN
(Indonesia)

CONTENTS

Foreword
David Suzuki

Only 500 human generations ago, all our ancestors lived a radically different, and now for almost all of the current generation of our species, an unfamiliar lifestyle — that of nomadic hunter-gatherer. Unencumbered by an economic system that encouraged the accumulation of material goods, these not-so-distant ancestors lived in balance with the natural world. Their knowledge of nature, acquired over countless generations of observation and insight, gave them the ability to survive.

For more than 99% of our species' existence, history chronicles almost imperceptible change punctuated by episodic catastrophes of plagues, floods, drought, and rare technological breakthroughs like the needle, bow and arrow, and pottery. The unprecedented explosive growth in our numbers and technological muscle-power began only a little over a century ago. Today, huge city-dwelling aggregates of people have become like blackholes, sucking energy and resources from the rest of the globe at a rate that exceeds the carrying capacity of the natural world.

In the past two decades, there has been an increase in the number and intensity of indicators telling us that something is drastically wrong — from a massive extinction crisis to atmospheric change and global pollution. Amidst these warnings has come a gradual recognition that we are grossly ignorant about the web of life that we are tearing apart so rapidly, and that we must relearn how to live more harmoniously with the land. Much of the repository of the working knowledge that our species needs to survive remains in tiny pockets of indigenous peoples who continue to retain a profound sense of connection with the land.

As a broadcaster, I have been privileged to encounter some remarkable peoples and cultures, including the the !Kung of the Kalahari Desert in

Botswana, and the Kaiapo Indians living along the Xingu River in the Amazon rainforest of Brazil. All possess an impressive understanding of the natural world that is the key to both their livelihood and their cultural and spiritual sense of purpose and identity. They know that they are deeply embedded in nature, and that if they lose that connection, they cease to exist as unique and special peoples.

The knowledge of aboriginal peoples is practical and set in the framework of the natural world, strikingly different from the compartmentalized information base of dominant, industrialized societies. Aboriginal perceptions are holistic in contrast with scientific insights which reveal properties of isolated parts of our surroundings and ultimately disconnect us further from the world.

I was struck by this fact when I recently visited the World Wildlife Fund's research station, near Manaus, Brazil. Several Ph.D's and students of herpetology demonstrated a remarkable ability to spot and capture tiny frogs in the middle of the night. Yet, when I asked one expert to identify a flower or an insect, he replied, "Don't ask me, I'm a herpetologist." In contrast, when I stayed with the Kaiapo Indians, deep in another part of the same Amazon rainforest, they had a name and a story for every single organism I pointed out. The knowledge indigenous peoples possess is far more profound and extensive than science provides, yet those very peoples are disappearing more rapidly than other species.

There are few people left on earth who are capable of living independently from the rest of the world, neither wanting, nor needing, the "civilized" way of life. They have become a mirror against which we can see ourselves and our belief systems. As the planet continues to fall before the insatiable demands of global economics, will we wipe out every last vestige of different worldviews?

Listen to Dawat. He is what we once were. He attests to a nobility that we must again become.

Penan Message

Dawat Lupung

The Penan speak with one voice.
This is the voice of one Penan.

What we say is, this forest,
 — we want to preserve it,
  because we have a good life here.

This land is our origins.
This land is our origins:
    the origin of our grandparents.
    the origin of our mothers and fathers.
    the origin of all those ancestors of ours long ago.

How can the government say this isn't our land?

I was raised to this age on this land:
    the place that supported our fathers,
    our mothers, our grandparents.
In this land,
    — in the Melinau river, in the Pakow river,
    in all these rivers I live.

In the Melinau, in the Pakow, these watersheds
    they provide me a way to live.

The government cannot open this land to be cut.
We belong here.
I myself belong here, having lived in all the old
   places of all of us living here since long ago.

Not long ago, we were happy.
Things were good.
Our fish were clean.
Our food was pure.
Our way of life staying in the forest was good.

As things are now, we are in difficulty.
The land is being destroyed.
Many open places.

We live by getting palm heart, by getting sago.
We eat different types of animals.
We are content making sago.
We miss eating all our foods from the land.
We don't like the logging companies.
The companies cheat us; they make our life hard.

We go out with blowpipe, get something,
    return…ah!
Content to eat, content with life.
That is what we like.
We go to look for palm hearts there.
Go make sago, get sago starch.
Ah, we are satisfied.

Land like this is what we really like.
There are trees, big, big trees like this.
The land looks good like this,
    — no tractor marks.
Big, big trees,
    — not fallen.
This is good.

From large trees like this,
    much fruit falls to the ground,
        — the food of pigs, the food of deer,
    food of all animals in the forest.

If the land is preserved like this,
    — all the hornbills, all the pigs, all animals
    happy to eat the fruits of the trees.

Satisfied life.
They eat the fruits.
We eat them.

Us, we too eat the fruits of this land.

There are many medicines,
    many hunting poisons here in the forest,
    — many, many here in the forest.

But, if the company comes, this is finished,
    — it is destroyed.
This, dead!
We don't like this.

These plants are our medicines.
If we ask for medicines from the government,
    they give us Panadol.
It is already spoiled. They give it to us.
The more we take, the sicker we become.
That is what we don't like.

If we eat just our medicines, good!
We eat Buhau, good!
We eat Ketiman, good!
Mia, good!
Laka Parak, good!

Here,
    — this vine is used by us
    to make packs, to make mats.
That plant there, we use to make sleeping mats,
    — big ones.
We use these things.
That is why we don't like it if they are destroyed.

That is why we need to save this land,
a big piece of land like this.

We are content to stay on this land,
to make our shelters in this forest.

This is a good life.

51

But if all these trees are gone,
    if there is no longer a way for us to stay here
    — hot!
We can't stand it hot.
It is painful.
You will see the illness, if the sun comes through.

If we have to settle by the rivers,
    — we don't have enough food.
Land, none.
Shelters, no good.

The water muddy, the fish dead.
Can't drink the water any more,
    — muddy, terrible, no good.
We don't like this.

Now even if we have enough to eat,
    it is not pure.
Even if we live long enough, we are unhappy.
Just a small illness, we are dead.

There is not enough to eat.
Many people will die,
    — no food.
Soon, many people die.

The company kills the trees.
We don't like it.
A terrible life then.
Can't live well any more.

The birds which fly high above, they flee!
If they hear the sound of the chainsaw,
    — they fly away.

If you look for them, they are no more.
The monkeys come, want to eat,
    hear sounds of logging,
    — they flee!
Far away from then on.
We go out to look for them,
    — none.
That is what we don't like.

Belengang (hornbills), other birds,
　　— they want to stay in big trees,
　　big trees like this!

Soon there will be no more large trees like this
　　for them to fly over or land on.
Their path is gone!
They wander all over.

They go far away.
We don't like this.

Trees that are cut down were once
    the shelter of hornbill,
    the home of gibbons,
    the home of langur,
    the home of every single kind of animal
    that lives up high.

Where is their home now?
Gone.
Finished!
No home for babui.
No more home for saai.
No more home for matui.
No home for kuai.

They don't like this.
We don't like this.

Our complaint is with those who look for
    tree trunks to get lots of money,
    — who cut down the big trees and
    sell them elsewhere.
They get dishonest money from selling trees
    like this.

The government makes many contracts.
The government is rich.
They make so many contracts, all the contracts
    we see in concessioned areas.
Don't you think they have so much money?
They have lots of money.

The logger is delighted.
He is eating the money from trees like this.
He is delighted to bulldoze a road,
    cut the trees, big, big trees,
    — get money!
His children, his wife, they are full.
They eat with the money they get from trees.

Our stomach is like this (thin).
Their stomach is out to here (fat).

I wanted to talk with the police about land to be
    saved for us to stay alive.
They don't want to talk.
They arrest me.
Here are the marks from being handcuffed when I
    was arrested by the government.
I want to talk, they hit me, they hit me like this.
That is the mistake of the government we
    don't like.

People who go to talk, go to jail.

Long ago during the British times,
    — hitting — there was none of that.
Penan were happy living in the headwaters.
The British came from down river
    with trade goods — shotguns, cartidges,
    cooking pots and machete like this, which we
    use to make our living.

How developed Penan are then.
How satisfied they are.

Now, the government gets angry with us.
Taib Mahud (Chief Minister for Sarawak) is angry.
Abdul Raham Yakub (former Prime Minister of
   Malaysia) is angry at us.

They say this is government land.
Land for Penan, there is none.

The government says we are animals,
    — like animals in the forest.

We are not animals in the forest.
We are Penan. Humans.
I myself know I am human.

Dead, dead, alive, alive,
    — It is decided by the government.
They don't know how to think like humans,
    don't know how to help people,
    people who are suffering,
    people who are poor.
Don't know how to act like humans.

We don't like the company to destroy
the forests any more:
they make the water muddy.
we become ill.
we get TB.
we get eye illness.
we get malaria.
we get killed on the bulldozer roads.

We want to see the land preserved.
Preserve a piece of land,
    — a very large area.

Up to how many acres? Up to how many acres?
Up to how many acres?
To enable hornbill,
    to enable deer,
    to enable pig,
    — so they will have a way to stay.

So friend, help us preserve this land as it is.
Help us so that they will divide,
    share the land with us,
    — not take it all away.

Ah, we would be grateful, thankful.
We would be happy if some land
    is saved for us Penan.

I want to say something else.
My name,
— Dawat Lupung.
I am Penan.
I am human.

Call for Action

Encountering Dawat

Thom Henley

It was hot, oppressively hot, April 7, 1989, when I first met Dawat Lupung at Batu Bungan, a Penan resettlement village in a remote part of the Borneo jungle. It was a setting of despair—a muddy riverbank and a cluster of shanties, their leprous facades patched with sheets of metal, plastic, and scavenged boards. Dawat's arrival turned out to be as refreshing and unexpected as the thunderstorm that cracked open the ominous late afternoon sky.

The storm came suddenly, violently, without warning. The forest beyond the settlement darkened, insects went silent, and the drop in air pressure became palpable. The rain began first in wild gusts and then in broad sheets that filled the horizon. Winds ripped plastic and rattled rusty sheet metal roofs. It was a torrential, tropical downpour. Raindrops fell in thunderous choruses, saturating the barren ground. Soon water the colour of the earth flooded the logged clearings that surrounded the settlement and poured over the riverbank transforming the Melinau River into a muddy torrent. The river grew rapidly, spreading over its banks, surging north to join the Tutoh and Baram Rivers, part of the network of affluents that wash the soils of Sarawak's cut-over rainforests into the South China Sea.

Penan children dressed in tattered clothes, some with half-closed, infected eyes, took shelter in open doorways and peered in bewilderment. For countless centuries their ancestors had been sheltered from tropical storms by the thick protective canopy of the forest. Now they, and thousands of other Penan in government camps, experienced an altogether different world: the full fury of the storms, the searing heat of the sun, the pain of hunger and starvation, the ravages of infectious disease, and the indignity of forced cultural assimilation.

A sudden gust of wind swept off the flank of Gunung Mulu, the mountain that arises from the centre of the Penan homeland, and tore a sheet of tin from the roof of one of the shanties. "Why does the government force us to live like this?" lamented a frightened Penan mother, nursing her child. "We don't know how to build houses." After translating her words of despair, our native interpreter gazed for a long time in silence over the squalid resettlement camp. Then as the rain finally began to let up he said quietly, "The government should be ashamed of this."

While we were still absorbed in this scene of desolation and human sadness, Dawat arrived from the distant forest bringing gifts and a smile.

I had come to Sarawak as part of an international team, the Endangered Peoples Project, a foundation based in Vancouver and San Francisco dedicated to the promotion of biological and cultural diversity. The mandate of our investigative team was straightforward.

For several years, international attention had focused on the plight of the Penan and other native peoples of Sarawak who were suffering immense deprivations as a result of the commercial logging that was destroying their customary forest lands. It was generally known that the rate of logging was increasing dramatically, and that the political resistance of the indigenous peoples was also escalating, yet there was very little visual documentation of the conflict.

The urgency of our journey was dictated by the response of the Sarawak government to international criticism of its forestry and human rights policies. In imposing an effective news blackout within Sarawak, and in orchestrating an international public relations campaign, designed both to deflect legitimate inquiry and to discredit its domestic critics, the government in Kuching indicated little interest in addressing, what were by all accounts, legitimate grievances and serious human rights violations. The logging was continuing at an ever accelerating rate.

In the fall of 1989 the USA-based Rainforest Action Network, a non-government environmental group coordinating efforts to preserve tropical rainforests, encouraged our organization to travel to Sarawak to obtain testimonials of the people most directly affected by the logging activities. In particular, our team sought to study and document through film, interviews, and photography, the current status of the Penan living in the upper reaches of the Baram River drainage in Sarawak's Fourth Division.

At the time of our arrival in Sarawak the situation remained highly charged. Harrison Ngau, the Kayan representative of Sahabat Alam (Friends of the Earth), Malaysia, and a vocal critic of the government's environmental policies, had been arrested under the Internal Securities Act of 1987. He remained under restraint in Marudi. Dozens of Penan and other indigenous peoples were also in Marudi facing criminal charges in District Court for their participation in logging road blockades.

Police permits were required for up river travel, even for those tourists who sought to venture into Gunung Mulu National Park. The Penan resettlements were off-limits to foreigners. Film equipment was suspect, and individuals caught taking photographs outside of their permit area risked both the confiscation of their film and deportation.

Thus we found ourselves somewhat surreptitiously sitting in a leaky shelter of Batu Bungan watching a young man wearing tattered trousers and carrying only a blowpipe cross the forest clearing and enter the settlement. Dawat Lupung did not act surprised to see us and, in fact, greeted us with the warmth of long lost friends. He presented each of us with a *jong*, a beautifully decorated rattan "dream bracelet" he had made.

We explained to Dawat and the other Penan the purpose of our visit. Dawat, in particular, grasped the significance of an opportunity to speak directly through the camera to people all over the world. Although we would later speak with many Penan and other Dayaks who had been more active and outspoken in upholding the rights of their people, the interview with Dawat turned out to be the most poignant. What made his testimony so moving was its simplicity and the evocative setting in which he spoke.

Dawat did not want to be interviewed in the dismal settlement of Batu Bungan. He and his friend Nyong Laing donned their traditional loincloths, took their blowpipes, dart quivers and parang knives, and led us by boat across the Melinau River to Gunung Mulu National Park. In the shelter of the forest, Dawat selected a place to speak his message to the world.

Crouching beside the flared buttress root of a giant tree that emerged above the jungle's canopy, Dawat was ready. To start the interview I asked: "Dawat, what does this forest mean to you; what would life be without this forest?" His friend Nyong, who had attended a Kayan school, knew enough English to pose the questions in Penan, but not enough to provide simultaneous translation.

Dawat took a deep breath and came wondrously alive. His eyes and arms almost danced as he made an impassioned plea for his forest and his people. For nearly an hour the power of the forest spoke through him, and when he ended there was an abrupt silence. For a few moments all of us sat quietly as the jungle sounds of distant birds and drumming cicadas filled the air. Although the details of what he said came only several months later when the interview was translated, we all sensed in our hearts that we had heard something both poetic and profound.

Dawat, born in 1963, was raised as a nomad in the forest of the Melinau River. He was in his teens when he first came in contact with people other than his own. Since then, he has watched the logging companies encroach further and further into his homeland, bringing with them the destruction of everything he holds sacred, including his foods, medicines, building materials, the temples of his gods, and the burial sites of his ancestors.

In 1976, with the stroke of a pen, the government made Dawat and his family squatters in their own homeland, and forced them to move outside of the boundaries of the newly created Gunung Mulu National Park. They were relocated to Batu Bungan, a government resettlement site, where they were expected to support themselves by making rattan baskets and mats to sell to tourists visiting the park. But instead of the better life the government had promised, they experienced hunger, malnutrition, infectious diseases, and a longing for their forest home and nomadic way of life.

When Dawat was 25, his father died when a tree accidentally fell on him while he was gathering *gaharu* resin. Dawat, the eldest son, became head of his family and responsible for hunting food. Dawat tried to support his mother and siblings, as well as his young wife and child, by walking for many days to hunt in the last remaining primary forest. More often than not, he returned empty handed.

In 1987, Dawat joined the Penan struggle to protect the last of their tribe's forest by helping erect peaceful blockades across logging roads. For his efforts, he was arrested, handcuffed, beaten by the police, and imprisoned for thirty days.

On July 11, 1989, in Washington, D.C., Dawat's testimonial was featured in a 20 minute, multi-media presentation, *The Penan — A Disappearing Civilization of Borneo*, which the Endangered Peoples Project presented to a special Congressional briefing on "Human Rights and Environmental Policy in Malaysia." In a setting not noted for passion, Dawat's moving testimony touched every heart, if only for a moment.

On November 6, 1989, exactly six months after he spoke to the world from his jungle home, Dawat Lupung became the recipient of the 1989 Reebok Human Rights Award, an award established to honour individuals who, early in their lives and against great odds, have significantly raised the awareness of human rights and exercised the freedom of expression. Dawat was unable to attend the December 5 award ceremony in Boston, Massachusetts, because he had to appear in court in Marudi to face criminal charges for blockading logging roads. Since Dawat was speaking for all of his people, the US$10,000 award money was forwarded, in his name, to the Penan Association to support the Penan in their efforts to save their homeland.

In February, 1990, ten months after our interview, Dawat, again, found himself in conflict with the logging companies. He tried to stop the desecration of his father's grave — to no avail. It was bulldozed.

Dawat Lupung can neither read nor write. His thumbprint is his only form of signature. In our culture, we tend to equate illiteracy with ignorance, and assume that only those formally educated and fluent with the written word can teach us. Perhaps it is time for peoples still part of an oral tradition to communicate to us through the medium we most respect — books.

This book is neither an anthropological monograph nor a journalistic analysis. It is a direct plea of a people and a forest in peril. I believe that Dawat speaks to us from the heart of nature itself. His voice is a voice for the trees, the birds, the wild pig, and every animal and plant that lives in this, the most complex forest in the world, so that "they will have a way to stay." He reminds us of what it means to belong, to be a part of a place, to be careful stewards of the earth, the only home we have.

I believe that the world community can and must grant the Penan and their forest a future, for only the continued existence of both ensures our own. The Penan's knowledge of plants and animals, potential medicines, and new food sources is but part of their gift to the world.

For if we listen, if we want to hear, these gentle forest dwellers may be able to give us the greatest gift of all by teaching us what it means to be truly human.

A Way to Stay

Wade Davis

In the time of our fathers, the tropical rainforests stood immense, inviolable, a mantle of green stretching across entire continents. That era is no more. Today in many parts of the tropics the clouds are made of smoke, the scents are of grease and lube oil, and the sounds one hears are of machinery, the buzz of chainsaws, and the cacophony of enormous reptilian earth movers hissing and moaning with exertion.

It is a violent overture, like the opening notes of an opera about war, a war between men and the land, a wrenching terminal struggle to make the latter conform to the whims and designs of the former. Each year an area of tropical forest more than three times the size of Belgium is laid waste. One species goes extinct every thirty minutes, and the rate is accelerating. Unless there is a dramatic global reduction in deforestation, more than a million species may become extinct within the next thirty years. Each disappearance marks not only the loss of an unique form of life, it represents the wanton sacrifice of an evolutionary possibility and its irrevocable severance from the stream of divine desire.

As the roads pierce the wild heart of the forests, the indigenous cultures suffer the most, the very people who have over the course of thousands of years developed an intimate knowledge of the land; men and women who, lacking the technology to transform the forest, chose instead long ago to understand it. Now, with dozens of tribal groups facing assimilation or destruction, we stand to lose in a single generation the accumulated wisdom of millennia.

There is at present no means of accurately evaluating the economic potential of the world's rainforests. But consider these startling statistics. At least 25% of modern drugs are derived from higher plants, and the majority of these were first used as medicines in a folk context. Annual worldwide sales of plant-derived pharmaceuticals currently total over $20 billion, and a great many of these drugs were first discovered by traditional healers. The gifts of the shaman and the herbalist, the curandero and the witch, include such critical drugs as digitoxin, vincristine, emetine, physostigmine, atropine, morphine, reserpine, d-tubo-curarine, and quinine.

An impressive 70% of all plants known to have anti-tumour properties have been found in tropical forests. Any one of these may lead to breakthroughs in the treatment of cancer. Yet, of an estimated 80,000 species of plants in the Amazon a mere 470 have been studied chemically and an astonishing 90% have not yet been subjected to even a superficial chemical analysis. The potential of this living pharmaceutical factory, like that of the immense forests of Southeast Asia and Borneo in particular, remains almost completely untapped.

The bounty of the world's rainforests is by no means limited to medicinal drugs. Of an estimated 75,000 edible plants found in nature a mere 150 enter world commerce and only 20, mostly domesticated cereals, stand between human society and starvation. Yet in the tropics there are wild trees that yield 650 pounds of oil rich seeds a year, a fruit with more vitamin C than oranges, a palm with more vitamin A than spinach, and another palm whose seeds contain 27% protein. There is a palm whose seed oil is indistinguishable from olive oil, and a tree producing resin which, if placed unprocessed into the fuel tank, will run a diesel engine. There are shrubs whose fruits contain natural compounds 300 times sweeter than sucrose, leaves coated with industrial grade waxes, seeds covered by brilliant dyes and pigments, lianas impregnated with biodegradable insecticides.

These then are the potential gifts of the rainforest — plants that heal, fruits and seeds that bring forth the foods we eat, magic plants that transport us to realms beyond our imaginings. Yet critically, in unveiling this indigenous knowledge, we must seek not only new sources of wealth but also a vision of life itself, a profoundly different way of living with the forest.

In Sarawak, the wisdom of an entire people is waiting to be heard. Numbering some 7,600, of whom perhaps a thousand remain deep in the forest following their ancient way of life, the Penan are one of the few truly nomadic rainforest societies of the earth. Related in spirit to the Mbuti pygmies of Zaire and the wandering Maku of the Northwest Amazon, the Penan never practised agriculture and depended instead on wild populations of sago palm for their basic carbohydrate supply. As hunters and gatherers they traditionally moved through the immense and remote forested uplands that give rise to the myriad affluents of the Baram River in Sarawak's Fourth Division; isolated populations ranged east across the frontier into Indonesian Kalimantan and north into Brunei.

Due in part to a remarkable variety of soil types, complex geomorphology, dramatic topographical gradients, and a broad range of climatic variation, the forests of the Penan are amongst the richest and most diverse ever to have evolved on the face of the earth. They may, in fact, represent one of the oldest living terrestrial ecosystems. Geologically and climatically, Borneo has remained remarkably stable, and this, together with a lack of volcanic activity or typhoons, has left the forests relatively undisturbed for millennia. Until this century, human impact has been slight and largely limited to the shifting fields of swidden agriculturalists who dwelt on the coast and in the broad river valleys of the interior. The hinterland has remained, until now, largely unscathed.

Represented within the traditional Penan homeland are all the major forest types to be found inland from the coast in Borneo. These forest communities are astonishingly diverse and harbour a great many endemic species. In Borneo, no fewer than 59 genera and 34% of all plant species are found only on the island. The fauna includes 30 unique birds and 39 endemic terrestrial mammals, as well as scattered populations of rare and endangered animals such as the Sumatran rhino and the orangutan. Botanical studies in Gunung Mulu National Park, which encompasses a small area in the heart of the Penan territory, have identified over 2,000 flowering plants including 120 species of palm, many of which are new to science. The limestone formations are especially rich. *Monophyllaea*, a rare genus of the African Violet family, is represented by no fewer than seven species, including six endemics. Of over 4,000 collections of fungi made by a single mycologist, perhaps half may be new species. Vegetation surveys yielded similarly impressive results. In the lowland mixed dipterocarp forests, botanists found 284 distinct tree species in three sample plots comprising only 1.2 hectares, a floristic diversity comparable to that of the most prolific areas of the Amazon.

For the Penan this forest is alive, pulsing, responsive in a thousand ways to their physical needs and their spiritual readiness. The products of the forest include roots that cleanse, leaves that cure, edible fruits and seeds, and magical plants that empower hunting dogs and dispel the forces of darkness. There are plants that yield glue to trap birds, toxic latex for poison darts, rare resins and gums for trade, twine for baskets, leaves for shelter and sandpaper, wood to make blowpipes, boats, tools, and musical instruments. For the Penan all of these plants are sacred, possessed by souls and born of the same earth that gave birth to the people.

Identifying both psychologically and cosmologically with the rainforest and depending on it for all their diet and technology, it is not surprising that the Penan are exceptionally skilled naturalists. It is the sophistication of their interpretation of biological relationships that is astounding. Not only do they recognize such conceptually complex phenomena as pollination and dispersal, they understand and accurately predict animal behaviour. They anticipate flowering and fruiting cycles of the edible forest plants, know the preferred foods of most forest animals, and may even explain where any animal prefers to pass the night. A recent and cursory examination of their plant lore suggested that the Penan recognize over 100 fruiting trees, some 50 medicinal plants, 8 dart poisons, and 10 plant toxins used to kill fish. These numbers probably represent but a fraction of their botanical knowledge.

These figures, impressive as they are, speak little of the spirit of the people. This one must sense in quiet moments, in gesture and repartee, and in dozens of representative actions that become symbols of the space through which these people live and die. To witness a headman distributing a gift of tobacco, the grace with which a hunter stalks his prey, the patience of children who know in the fibre of their being that all the gifts of the forest are to be shared — these moments tell you something of what it means to be Penan.

The rate of deforestation in Malaysia is the highest in the world. In 1983, Malaysia accounted for 58% of the total global export of tropical logs, with over 90% of the wood going to Japan, Taiwan, and South Korea. By 1985, three acres of forest were being cut every minute of every day. With primary forests in peninsular Malaysia becoming rapidly depleted, the industry increasingly has turned to Sarawak. Between 1963 and 1985, 30% of the forested land of Sarawak was logged, and within the last decade the area of land cut each year increased 500%. In 1985, 270,000 hectares were logged, providing a full 39% of the national production and generating over US$1.7 billion in foreign exchange. Today another 5.8 million hectares — 60% of Sarawak's forested land — is held in logging concessions. Should current rates of cut continue, another 28% of Sarawak's forests will be logged within the next decade. In the Fourth Division which contains much of the traditional homeland of the Penan, 72% of the forest is slated to be felled.

Datuk James Wong, Minister of the Environment and Tourism and holder of one of the larger timber concessions in Sarawak, believes that "logging is good for the forest," and maintains that within five years of selective harvest there is no discernable difference between a logged and a primary forest. Studies produced by the UN's Food and Agriculture Organization (FAO) and the World Wildlife Fund (WWF) suggest, by contrast, that selective logging damages perhaps 50% of the residual stands, removes 46% of the natural cover, and seriously damages soils when over 30% of the ground surface is exposed. The Penan, meanwhile, know only that the silt in the rivers blinds their fish, the sago, rattan, palms, lianas and fruits lie crushed on the forest floor, that the wild pig flee with the hornbill, and that every time a tree falls in the forest, it brings with it a star.

If the Penan are to have the opportunity to choose their own destiny, their forest homeland must be protected. Moreover, the interests of the Penan as well as those of the neighbouring Dayak peoples must be balanced with the need to protect the biological integrity of the land now delineated by Gulung Mulu National Park. The creation of a Biosphere Reserve is an obvious and important solution, one that is particularly appropriate to the situation in Sarawak. First promoted in 1974 as an unique land designation by the United Nations Educational, Scientific, and Cultural Organization (UNESCO), a Biosphere Reserve combines forest preservation with the subsistence needs of surrounding communities. Typically a Biosphere Reserve consists of a series of concentric zones, each having a different land use mandate. At the heart of the Reserve is invariably a core of permanently protected forest. Moving outward from this centre are a series of increasingly intensive utilisation zones. In the first zone, indigenous peoples are permitted to hunt, collect medicinal plants, and harvest natural products. In the next zone, people may farm and gather wood. Settlement occurs in a third zone which acts to buffer the Reserve from encroaching development.

Local initiative and the direct involvement of national and regional authorities are critical to both the establishment and maintenance of a Biosphere Reserve. Fortunately, in Sarawak it appears that both conditions may be met. In October 1987 an intra-governmental report submitted by the State Task Force on Penan Affairs to the Sarawak State Cabinet Committee on Penan Affairs called for the establishment of two Biosphere Reserves for the nomadic Penan, one to be located in the Baram District in the Tutoh-Magoh-Kuba'an river system and the other in the Limbang district on the Sepayang River.

At a February 12, 1990 meeting, the Penan Association endorsed the Biosphere Reserve concept, substantially increasing the proposed boundaries to surround Gunung Mulu National Park and include a large portion of the northeast section of the Fourth Division, an area encompassing approximately 18,000 square kilometres.

A vital section of the Penan resolution called for the legal recognition of the customary land rights of all indigenous peoples of Sarawak. To date, the Sarawak government has neither taken steps toward implementing the recommendations of the State Task Force on Penan Affairs, nor officially endorsed the Biosphere Reserve concept as a possible solution to the conflict.

In Sarawak the representatives of the government often say that environmentalists and anthropologists want to sequester indigenous peoples in living zoos, thus robbing them of the opportunity to enter the "mainstream of civilization." In fact, proponents of a Biosphere Reserve seek only to guarantee the Penan a choice. That many Penan still desire to pursue their traditional subsistence activities is evident in the numerous public statements of the Penan Association, a fact that has been acknowledged by government officials. According to Environment and Tourism Minister Datuk James Wong, the Penan "have always posed a problem as they choose to live as wandering nomads in the jungles. They pose a dilemma to the government... Efforts to persuade them to settle down is (sic) almost an impossible task. Nevertheless, the Government has and is still doing its best to do so."

"No one," Wong stated recently, "has the ethical right to deprive the Penan of their right to socio-economic development and assimilation into the mainstream of Malaysian society." This statement is true, but its corollary is equally correct. Penan, like all other indigenous groups of Sarawak, surely have the right to determine the degree to which they become incorporated into the Malaysian society, even as they have an obligation to their own children to protect the integrity of their civilization. For a nomadic culture to cease to move is essentially to die.

In another memorable quote, James Wong touched upon the dark undercurrent of the confrontation. "We don't want them," he said of the Penan, "running around like animals. Shouldn't they be taught to be hygienic like us and eat clean food?" One struggles to reconcile such a statement with an image of the Penan bathing in their clear streams, or in the forest, manipulating their plants with a dexterity equal to that of a laboratory chemist.

One recalls a morning in which a group of visitors shared their "clean food" with Asik Nyelik, a nomadic Penan from beyond the headwaters of the Baram River. The night before, Asik had slept poorly in a bed and that morning at breakfast, looking rather tired, he sat uncomfortably in a chair. He drank from a glass of water as would a deer, dipping his mouth to the surface. Then came breakfast, a depressing offering of cold canned beans, a sorry looking fried egg, and a slice of tinned sausage. Asik politely looked around the table, then to his plate, then once again at the people eating this food. He rotated his plate, hunting perhaps for an angle from which the food might appear palatable. Backing away from the table with a look of sincere pity, he slipped out of the building and into the forest. An hour later smoke rose from the edge of the forest and Asik was found hunched over a fire, slowly roasting a mouse deer that he had killed with a blade.

Several nights later there was a full moon. It reminded Asik of a story he had heard about some people who had travelled there and returned with dust and rocks. He asked if the story was true. Told that it was, after a moment of silence he asked, "Why bother?"

E.O. Wilson, renowned Harvard biologist, has said that the 20th century will not be remembered for its wars or its technological advances but rather as the era in which men and women stood by and either passively endorsed or actively supported the massive destruction of biological and cultural diversity on the planet. Our prosperity has been purchased at a cost that may well fill our descendants with shame.

Sensitivity to nature is not an innate attribute of the Penan. It is a consequence of adaptive choices that have resulted in the development of highly specialized perceptual skills. But those choices in turn spring from a comprehensive view of nature and the universe in which man and woman are perceived as but elements inextricably linked to the whole. It is another worldview altogether, one in which man stands apart, that now threatens their forest and our world with devastation.

Perhaps the greatest gift of the Penan will be their contribution to a dialogue between these two worldviews such that folk wisdom may temper and guide the inevitable development processes that today ride roughshod over much of the earth.

Wade Davis.

Beyond the Images
Wade Davis and Thom Henley

Front Cover — Penan hunters stalking prey

Detecting every sound and movement, Dawat Lupung and Nyong Laing move silently and swiftly through the primary forest's understorey. Like all nomadic Penan hunters, they travel light, carrying only a *keleput,* a blowpipe of bored hardwood with an *atap,* or hunting spear, lashed to its tip. The poison darts for the blowpipe are carried in a *tello,* a bamboo container attached to a waist belt. A machete, or *po-e,* and a small knife, *nahan,* complete the set of tools and weaponry traditionally carried by Penan hunters.

The principal and often only article of clothing worn by Penan men is a loincloth or *chawat. Chawats* were first made of barkcloth, *kulit kayu,* but are today fashioned from up to five meters of cloth obtained by trade with the neighbouring Kayan and Kenyah tribespeople, or from coastal Malay and Chinese merchants. Any design is acceptable, but the red, blue, and white banded *chawat* worn by Nyong is the more traditional pattern and may, in fact, have been inspired by the British flag during the century of colonial rule.

Though many semi-settled and nomadic Penan are now adopting western dress, the loincloth has considerable advantages in the hot wet rainforest. By day it is cool and, leaving the limbs free, it permits the silent stalking of game. Relatively easy to clean, the long lengths of cloth favoured by some Penan double as blankets in the surprisingly cool Borneo nights.

Page 2 — Sarawak rainforest seen through a spider's web

The rainforests of Borneo comprise a part of what many believe to be the oldest and richest terrestrial ecosystem on earth. The forests of Southeast Asia originated long before the extinction of the dinosaurs and have flourished continuously for approximately 180 million years. During the Pleistocene glaciations, when global climate change transformed much of the equatorial African and Amazonian rainforest to dryland savannah, Southeast Asia's rainforests, surrounded by water, retained their moist climatic regime. Millions of years of evolution, uninterrupted by major climatic transformations, has resulted in perhaps the most diverse and complex forest on earth.

The biodiversity of tropical rainforests is astounding. A hectare of temperate woodland usually contains no more than a dozen tree species. In the tropics the number might well reach 300. The insect fauna in the tropical rainforests has been estimated to include thirty million species. One entomologist found more species of ants in a single tropical tree stump than had been reported for all of Great Britain. Another found 1200 species of beetles in the crowns of 19 individuals of a single species of tree. Borneo is home to over a thousand species of cicadas. Two square kilometres of tropical rainforest may support 23,000 forms of life.

This lush ecosystem is maintained by a complex process of nutrient recycling. In the temperate zone, the periodicity of the seasons results in the accumulation of rich organic topsoils which serve as a reservoir for up to 80% of the nutrients of the ecosystem. In the tropical forest, by contrast, the biological wealth is stored in the living canopy. With constant high humidity and annual temperatures hovering around 27 degrees Celsius, bacteria and microorganisms break down plant matter virtually as soon as the leaves hit the forest floor. With the aid of microbial fungi, a complex mat of tiny rootlets absorbs the nutrients, which are immediately recycled into the living forest itself, an exceedingly complex mosaic of thousands of interacting and interdependent organisms.

Despite the abundance of biological life, the tropical ecosystem is unexpectedly fragile and in many respects a counterfeit paradise. It is quite literally a castle of immense sophistication built on a foundation of sand. The soil is the problem — in many instances there virtually is none. In any other part of the world, these lands might be deserts. Only rainfall and temperature insulate the forest from the poor quality of the soil and thus permit the luxuriant growth.

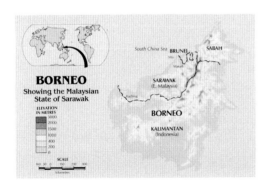

Page 4 — Map

Straddling the equator and stretching 800 miles east to west and 600 miles north to south, Borneo is the third largest island on earth. Six major rivers and literally hundreds of smaller streams drain the isolated centre of the island where the mountains of the Kalimantan highlands rise to over 13,000 feet. Eighty percent of Borneo is blanketed by extraordinarily rich tropical rainforest. Politically the island is claimed by three nations. Indonesian Kalimantan encompasses the southern two-thirds, while to the north the small oil rich sultanate of Brunei is flanked by the Malaysian states of Sarawak and Sabah.

Sarawak joined the Federation of Malaysia in 1963. Before that, it had been under the direct or indirect influence of the English for over a hundred years. In 1841, a British adventurer named James Brooke, supported by the ships of the Royal Navy, established what became a virtual trading monopoly in Sarawak and laid the foundations of a remarkable family dynasty. Known as the White Rajahs of Sarawak, the male scions of the Brooke family ruled until 1946 when, in the twilight of the British Empire, Vyner Brooke ceded control of Sarawak to Britain. The terms under which the Crown Colony of Sarawak joined the Malaysian Federation in 1963 were precise and historically significant. All matters of defense, security, taxation, and control of the vast petroleum reserves were placed under the authority of the federal government in Kuala Lumpur. The State government of Sarawak, however, retained complete control of forest resources, and all matters related to land tenure and utilisation.

Today, Malaysia is a country of 15 million, a net producer of oil and the world's leading exporter of tin, palm oil, rubber, pepper, and tropical timber. Sarawak encompasses roughly 38% of Malaysian territory and has a population of approximately 1.2 million. Within this state there are some 27 distinct ethnic groups. The Melanau and Malay comprise a fifth of the population. Thirty percent are Chinese or recent immigrants from throughout Southeast Asia. Close to half of the population, however, is Dayak, a collective term that refers to the members of more than a dozen indigenous peoples including the Iban, Bidayuh, Kenyah, Kayan, Kedayan, Murut, Punan, Bisayah, Kelabit, and Penan. The Penan, who live in northeastern Sarawak, currently number approximately 7,600, of whom 25% are settled. The remainder are semi-settled or nomadic and depend upon the rainforest for most or all of their material and dietary needs. Of the estimated 100,000 indigenous peoples who roamed the forests of Sarawak at the turn of this century, only the nomadic Penan remain. Globally they represent one of the very few extant societies of wandering tropical rainforest peoples.

Page 6 — Deep in the rain-forest a Borneo orangutan nurses her infant

The Borneo orangutan is the largest and most intelligent of all the arboreal apes. Unlike the more social gibbons of Southeast Asia, and the gorillas and chimpanzees of Africa, orangutans live largely solitary lives. Officially protected, the Borneo orangutan is seriously threatened by current logging practices. Disoriented by machinery and logging activities, orangutans frequently seek refuge in emergent trees and are killed when these trees are fallen. Infant orangutans, cushioned from the impact by their mothers, sometimes survive and are taken as pets. Most soon die. A fortunate few are placed into rehabilitation centers and later reintroduced to the wild. Survival rates for these reintroduced animals are not known.

Page 9 — Pinnacles — Gunung Mulu National Park

The traditional homeland of the Penan is a varied and magical landscape of forest and soaring mountains, dissected by crystaline rivers and impregnated by the world's most extensive network of caves and underground passages. Carved by wind and water from the extensive formation of Melinau limestone that underlies much of Gunung Mulu National Park, the Pinnacles are one of the most dramatic geological features in Borneo. Located at the northern end of Gunung Api at about 1200 meters, they emerge from the forest canopy, fluted and imposing, like perfectly formed blades of glass produced in a workshop of the gods.

Page 10 — Portrait of Dawat Lupung

The Penan are people of the rainforest. According to one of their myths of origin, in the beginning man and woman were alone and knew nothing of reproduction and rebirth. There was a tree in the deep forest that had a wide hole in its trunk, just above the ground. Nearby was another tree that had a large branch that pointed to the cavity in the first tree. One day a storm blew, and the man and woman watched as the two trees twisted in the wind, until suddenly the branched tree fell onto the other, penetrating the cavity again and again as the wind buffeted the forest. Man and woman came together, imitating the trees and thus were born the children that gave rise to the Penan.

Born of the forest and dependent on it for every aspect of their material lives, the Penan long ago embarked on a journey that knew no end. Fearful of the heat of the sun, ignorant of the seas, insulated from the heavens by the branches of the canopy, their entire cognitive and spiritual world became based on the forest. Distance and time became measured not in hours or miles but rather in the quality of the experience itself. With good hunting a journey is short, though it might be measured by a European in weeks. A long arduous journey is one that exposes the Penan to the sun. When a Penan enters a stretch of unknown forest he or she must *mal cun uk*, or "follow our feelings," a process that defies analysis but which allows the Penan to accomplish phenomenal feats of orienteering. As the Penan explain: "The earthworm can go hungry and the mouse deer become lost in the forest, but never we Penan."

The length of a journey is determined in the moment, by the discovery of wild fruits, a stand of sago, the chance to kill a wild pig. The passage of time is measured by the activities of insects, the sweat bees that emerge two hours before dusk, the black cicadas that electrify the forest at precisely six in the evening. If there is a pattern to the Penan migration, it is determined by the sacred growth cycle of the sago palm. It is a journey that may take twenty years to complete, an itinerary first described by the ancestors at a time when the earth was young and still wet with the innocence of birth.

Page 13 —
Dawat Lupung and Nyong Laing in the forest

Like most nomadic peoples of the rainforest, the Penan are egalitarian and non-hierarchical. Their social structure is based on an extended network of obligations, mediated by a host of kin ties and a complex naming system that links the generations even as it aligns the living with the dead. In the absence of social stratification, there are no specialists. Although certain individuals may be more talented than others at specific tasks, the hunting and gathering adaptation demands self-sufficiency and each person must be capable of participating in every societal activity.

Thus Dawat speaks to us not as a chief or tribal authority, but merely as a Penan who in his person embodies the collective spirit of his people.

Page 14 —
Deer Cave and the Borneo forest at sunset

The Penan trace their origins in the Borneo rainforest to the dawn of time. Archaeological investigations in the Niah caves, which are situated within Penan territory in northern Sarawak, have discovered the oldest carbon dated human remains in Southeast Asia and have documented 50,000 years of nearly continuous occupation ending in 250 BC. The relationship between the original inhabitants of these caves and the contemporary Proto-Malay speaking Dayaks is uncertain. Most anthropologists believe that the ancestors of the Dayaks originated on the Southeast Asian mainland, gradually moving down the Malay peninsula some 4,000 years ago, displacing or subduing the original inhabitants of what is now Indonesia, the Philippines, and Malaysia. Indeed, the mythologies of most indigenous peoples of Sarawak speak of ancient migrations from other parts of Southeast Asia. The Penan, by contrast, say simply: "This land is our origin." Penan alone, they maintain, eschewed the cult of the seed and remained true to the wandering ways of their ancestors.

Page 17 — A Penan hunter in the notch cut from a living tree to yield wood for blowpipes, Penan woman weaving palm leaves, and native palm used for roofing.

The Penan believe that the rainforest and its bounty were given to them by the Creator, the God *Balei Nge Butun*. Their biological adaptation, together with their spiritual beliefs, demand that they exploit the forest in a sustainable manner. Central to their world view is a sacred

obligation to bequeath to the following generations a healthy forest fully capable of providing life to its human inhabitants.

For the Penan, the forest is alive, the trees blessed with spirits, the animals imbued with magical powers. One may take from a tree, as this Penan elder has done in obtaining wood to make a blowpipe, but it is taboo to kill any large tree. To do so is to release its spirit, the *baleh*, and to expose one's people to dire consequences. For Penan, every forest sound is an element of a language of the spirit. Trees bloom when they hear the lovely song of the barethroated *krankaputt*. Bird calls heard from a certain direction bear good tidings, the same sounds heard from a different direction may be a harbinger of ill. Entire hunting parties may be turned back by the call of a banded kingfisher, the cry of a bat hawk. Other birds like the *ichit*, the spider hunter, summon the hunter to the kill. Before embarking on a long journey the Penan must see a white-headed hawk flying from right to left, they must hear the call of the crested rain bird, and the doglike sound of the barking deer.

To walk in God's forest is to tread through an earthly paradise where there is no separation between the sacred and the profane, the material and the immaterial, the natural and the supernatural. Yet always one moves with caution. When a Penan hunter leaves camp, he must never tell anyone of his intentions for fear of warning his prey. Instead he says *"tie neet neet,"* which translates literally to "we're going to the forest to pull back our foreskin." Similarly, a woman going fishing may say *"muee loto,"* an expression which means "to go and wipe our rear ends." Wonderfully funny, these salacious euphemisms are also indicative of the intimate relationship maintained between the Penan and every aspect of their rainforest homeland. As the Penan elder nestled in the living tree trunk explains: "The land is sacred; it belongs to the countless numbers who are dead, the few who are living, and the multitudes of those yet to be born. How can the government say that all untitled land belongs to itself, when there had been people using the land even before the government itself existed?"

Page 18 — Melinau River

The Melinau River, flowing through the Melinau Gorge, is part of an ancient trade and travel route that connects the Tutoh and Limbang watersheds. The route has been travelled by the Penan for thousands of years. The Melinau, now protected within the boundaries of Gunung Mulu National Park, is one of Sarawak's few remaining clear flowing rivers. Commercial logging and related activities have left sixty percent of Sarawak's rivers seriously polluted with diesel fuel, sawdust, mud, industrial toxins, and miscellaneous debris.

Soil erosion and the increased siltation and turbidity of the rivers is arguably the most serious environmental impact of logging. The most conservative estimates suggest that the removal of the forest canopy results in a thirty fold increase in soil loss on a given acreage of tropical land. A United Nations study in the Ivory Coast concluded that on land with a seven percent slope, soil erosion was negligible on forested land (0.03 tons/ha./yr.) but increased dramatically to 90 tons/ha./yr. on cultivated land and 138 tons/ha./yr. on land stripped of vegetation. Studies in peninsular Malaysia suggest that soil loss on logged land may be as high as 79 tons/ha./yr. Other Malaysian studies indicate that logging operations followed by agricultural exploitation of forest lands may cause a 200 fold increase in the sediment load of streams.

Page 21 — Mutang Tuo standing in the midst of a clump of sago

Language is the filter through which the soul of a people reaches into the material world. In Penan there are forty words for sago, and no words for goodbye or thank you. In a forest of such abundance, in a culture in which sharing is an involuntary reflex, in a life of endless wandering, certain words have no relevance. Certain concepts have no meaning. For the Penan, land is a living entity, imbued with spiritual meaning and power, and the notion of ownership of land, of fragile documents granting a human the right to violate the earth, is an impossible idea.

For all Dayak peoples, the concept of private ownership of land did not exist. In the agricultural societies customary law dictated that the community as a whole controlled the resource base. Individual proprietory rights were automatically granted to those who worked the land, provided they fulfilled the incumbent ritual and ecological obligations. This principle of land stewardship is enshrined in traditional law or *adat*, a concept that has moral, legal, and religious implications. The subversion of this philosophy, the imposition of a foreign notion of land tenure, and the wresting of control of the land from the indigenous peoples are three dominant themes that have molded Sarawak history since the time of the British.

The benchmark for resource management in Sarawak is Forest Ordinance 1953 which divides the land into Permanent Forests and Stateland Forests. The former come under the control and protection of the Forestry Department and are expected to satisfy the forestry needs of the state indefinitely. Stateland Forests are available for agriculture and other uses. As of 1985, 34%, or approximately 33,000 sq. km., of Sarawak's 95,000 sq. km. of forested land had been designated Permanent Forest. The remainder, some 62,000 sq. km., constituted Stateland Forest. On Stateland Forests logging is allowed by permit and there are no restrictions on permissible yields and no management activity by the Forestry Department.

Permanent Forests are of three types: Forest Reserves, Protected Forests, and Communal Forests. Forest Reserves are set aside as permanent sources of timber. Entry is limited to those licenced for a specific extractive task. Indigenous people are not allowed to harvest or gather any resource of any kind in the Forest Reserves. In Protected Forests, indigenous customary tenure is similarly forbidden, though indigenous peoples may hunt, fish, and forage, provided they obtain a permit from the Forestry Department. Communal Forests are intended to supply the domestic needs of the traditional communities and acknowledge the customary system of land tenure specifically recognized by Sarawak law. Communal Forests exist at the discretion of the Minister of Forests and may be revoked at any time. As of December 31, 1984, Communal Forests made up only 56 sq.km., or 0.17 % of Sarawak's Permanent Forests. As Evelyn Hong writes in *Natives of Sarawak*:

"The creation of Permanent Forests is really to 'protect' large areas of the forests from being claimed by the natives, so that the areas can be made available to logging companies to exploit timber, although in a manner more controlled and regulated than in the free-for-all situation prevailing on the Stateland Forests."

Because Sarawak law technically provides for the rights of those Dayaks who work the land, the government has consistently maintained that the non-agricultural Penan have no legitimate claim to customary lands, and cannot exercise any traditional rights unless they settle down and become farmers. Hence the Penan are placed in the impossible position of having to abandon completely their traditional way of life in order to obtain recognition of their customary rights.

Page 22 — Mutang Tuo picking Mulu apples and holding a catch of fish

Although a complete study of Penan ethnobotany has yet to be done, it is known that the Penan identify and consume more than a hundred wild fruits, numerous species of fungi, and many types of wild greens and edible palms. During the fruiting season neighbouring groups of Penan gather to feast on the local abundance. In this image, Mutang Tuo, of Long Iman, is seen gathering *leposo*, known also as Mulu apple. It, like many understory trees of the Borneo rainforest, flowers and fruits from the trunk, an adaptation, in many instances, to bat pollination. The Mulu apple has a pleasant tart flavour and is valued by the Penan as both food and medicine. Employed to improve sinus congestion, it is also considered particularly beneficial for pregnant women.

Penan recognize and eat more than thirty species of fish. Many of these are fruit eaters, dependent on the trees that overhang the myriad rivers of the Penan homeland. To catch these fish, the Penan toss small pebbles that mimic falling fruit, and then cast their nets as the fish rush to the decoy. Alternatively, the Penan may employ one of as many as ten biodegradable fish poisons which they derive by crushing leaves, stems, roots, and/or fruits of certain forest plants. Placed in slow moving bodies of water, these plant materials release chemical compounds that interact with the gills, inhibit respiration, ultimately causing death by suffocation. The affected fish float to the surface and are readily gathered. The environmental impact of these plant toxins is slight and localized and their use does not cause permanant harm to the aquatic ecosystem.

The fish displayed in this photograph were caught in a remote tributary of the Silat River, a drainage that is scheduled to be logged in the near future.

Page 25 —
Sago gathering and processing techniques

The most important staple of the Penan is the starch gathered and prepared from six different species of wild sago palm: *Uvud, Jakah, Anau, Leseh, Bohok*, and *Iman*. Sago is to the Penan what wheat is to the West and rice to the East. Without this readily available basic source of carbohydrate, the Penan would be incapable of maintaining their nomadic way of life. To them, sago is not considered a vegetable; it is a form of meat, and hunting it is as integral to Penan life as is the pursuit of wild game.

Of all the sago palms, the Penan prefer *iman, Caryota no,* for it produces a sweet flour in abundance. Second choice would be *leseh, Caryota mitis,* which yields a similar flour but in less quantity. Third choice would be *jaka, Arenga undulatifolia.* Their main source, however, is *uvud, Eugeissona utilis,* a wild palm which grows commonly in dense groves, particularly on hillsides throughout the Penan territory.

In the photograph on the left, Anyie Katan of Long Tikan is seen on an elevated platform that allows him to harvest the upper trunk of a sago palm, while avoiding the sharp spines of the base. To ensure that the plant will regenerate, great care is taken to avoid damaging the roots. Once the trunk has been fallen, it is cut into manageable sections and carried to an appropriate place for processing, generally a stream or nearby body of water. The sections of trunk are split longitudinally and pounded with a wooden mallet called a *palu* until the soft inner pith fluffs up. The empty shell of the palm trunk, the *banggah,* is discarded and the fibrous pulp, known as *papah,* is then placed on a finely woven rattan mat held on a low four foot square frame, as shown in the second photograph. A worker climbs onto the top mat to knead the pulp with his feet, while another pours water onto the frame. The starch mixes with the water, filters through the rattan and forms a fine brown sludge which is collected from the surface of the lower mat. Later, usually back at camp, the extract is smoked to remove excess moisture and produce the actual sago flour.

The entire process generally takes one day and produces enough sago flour to last a family four days. The Penan consume an average of one *gantang* (approximately 3.5 kg) of sago flour per person per week, a quantity that requires a family of six to cut and process six sago palms each week.

Depending on the palm species used and the means of preparation, cooked sago has a taste and texture ranging from bland and glutinous to rich and meaty. The common method of preparation involves mixing the sago with a little water and heating it over a fire until the flour coagulates. The cooked flour in its gluey consistency is called *linut*. Cooked simply with *babui*, it is known as *siigo*. Wrapped with pig meat in leaves and roasted over a fire, it is called *grumut*.

Gathering sago is the purest expression of Penan life. A meal of rice, they say, leaves them hungry in an hour, but a plate of sago fills their stomachs for days. Sago can be harvested, prepared and eaten on the same day. Rice cultivation requires exhaustive work, months of waiting and permanent settlements with adequate granaries for storage. Faced with such a choice, the Penan ask, who would choose to settle down?

Page 26 — Mutang Tuo launching dart from blowpipe

With a powerful blast of air from his lungs, Mutang Tuo fires a poisoned dart at a mouse deer on the edge of a clearing. Completely dependent on the forest for food, the Penan are widely acknowledged by other Dayak peoples as being the best trackers and hunters, the undisputed masters of the blowpipe.

The blowpipe, or *keleput*, is a marvel of indigenous technology. Though less useful than a shotgun in the dense undergrowth of a secondary forest, in the open primary forest its efficiency is unsurpassed. A blowpipe is lighter than a shotgun, manufactured from forest materials, and its ammunition is readily replaced. The darts kill silently, allowing a hunter in certain instances to bag several animals or, alternatively, to take a second shot should his first miss.

Though several species may be used, the preferred material is the hard, straight grained wood of the *nyagang* tree. In making the blowpipes, a square length of wood 2 to 2.5 meters long is cut from a living tree and subjected to preliminary carving. A high platform is then constructed for the painstaking process of boring the shaft. Standing on the platform, the blowpipe maker uses a long narrow iron bore to drill vertically through the length of the weapon, occasionally pausing to pour water into the hole to float up the sawdust and cool the bore. Once the drilling is complete, the outside of the weapon is rounded and then given a fine finish with the *bekela* leaf, a botanical substitute for sandpaper. The entire process may take weeks to complete. Once the blowpipe is finished, an iron blade is lashed to its tip and the weapon doubles as a spear.

The blowpipe technology utilises half a dozen forest plants. The dart quiver is made of bamboo, darts are fashioned from the stem of the *nibong* palm, and the cone-shaped appendage at the base of the dart that fits precisely the bore of the weapon is carved from the pith of sago. These appendages are carefully carved on a wooden bodkin and stored in a gourd container. Two types of darts are used. A *tahat* is a straight, wooden projectile used chiefly to kill small prey — birds, squirrels, lizards, snakes, frogs, and other amphibians. A metal tipped dart, the *belat*, is employed for larger game such as monkeys and mouse deer. In every instance poison is applied to the tip of the dart.

On sighting prey, the Penan hunter becomes still, and then begins a series of slow, cautious movements. A poisoned dart, taken from the bamboo quiver lashed to his waistband, is inserted into the mouthpiece end of the blowpipe. Holding the weapon steady, the hunter inhales, filling his powerful lungs with air, and then pauses to take final aim. The accuracy of these weapons is such that targets the size of small coins may be struck from 25 meters; small birds are readily taken from the canopy of the forest. Superb hunters, the Penan sometimes load two darts into the blowpipe, firing them in rapid succession with two blasts of the same breath. Once an animal has been struck by a poison dart, the Penan stalk the prey cautiously, waiting for 10 to 30 minutes for the animal to succumb to the toxin.

In hunting larger game such as deer or wild boar, the Penan generally use dogs, and they slay their prey with spears. The meat is always divided evenly among the extended kin group. The greatest transgression in Penan society is *see hun*, a term that translates roughly as a failure to share. Dependent on the forest for life, and each other for survival, the Penan have, in effect, institutionalised individual generosity as a means of insulating the group as a whole from the inevitable uncertainties inherent in a hunting and gathering way of life.

In Penan society proper social behavior is learned by example rather than by rigorous discipline, and the importance of sharing is instilled in children from the earliest age. Young boys mastering the use of a blowpipe, for example, are encouraged to carefully divide the cooked meat from the smallest of prey, allotting equal portions to all the other children. In one instance, a young Penan youth who had gone hungry for several days, killed a pygmy squirrel, a *tele*, the world's smallest squirrel, which he cooked and consumed alone. His failure to share provoked not anger but laughter on the part of the adults. They simply bestowed on the boy the name *tele*, so that he would never forget his transgression.

Page 29 — Flared buttress of a towering emergent tree

Due to the unique nutrient regime of tropical forests, up to 90% of tree roots are found within the top ten centimetres of the forest floor. The flared buttresses are a structural adaptation that enables certain emergent trees to withstand the high winds that regularly sweep the canopy. When a tropical forest giant like this blows over, it cuts a swath in the forest, levelling dozens of smaller trees and dragging with it others whose crowns are interwoven by thick, woody lianas. The opening created in the canopy provides opportunities for a myriad of sun loving plants. This process, by which old giants die and new growth emerges to take their place, is part of the natural cycle of the forest and is not comparable to the ravages exacted on the land by the logging activities of man.

The indiscriminate removal of the tropical forest cover over a large area sets in motion a chain reaction of destruction. Temperatures increase dramatically, relative humidity falls, rates of evapotranspiration drop precipitously, and the mycorrhizal mats that interlace the roots of the forest trees facilitating the absorption of nutrients dry up and die. With the cushion of vegetation gone, the torrential rains create erosion which leads to further loss of nutrients and chemical changes in the soil itself. In certain deforested parts of the tropics, the precipitation of iron oxides in leached exposed soils has resulted in the deposition of miles upon miles of lateritic clay, a rock-hard pavement of red earth from which not a weed will grow.

Selected logging as practiced even in the most closely monitored stands in Sarawak has a long term and detrimental environmental impact. Studies published by the United Nations Food and Agriculture Organization (FAO) and the World Wildlife Fund (WWF) suggest that selective logging damages 50% of the residual stands, removes 46% of the natural cover, and seriously damages soils when over 30% of the ground surface is exposed. Related studies have concluded that if a mere ten trees are fallen per hectare, nearly half of the area will be adversely affected. In addition, the construction of roads, landings and trails permanently alters 12% of the total forest area. The estimate for the time necessary for the selectively logged forest to recover is forty years, far shorter than the twenty-five year rotation employed in the most closely managed stands of mixed dipterocarp hill forest in Sarawak. According to the World Bank 1978 Forestry Sector Policy Paper: "There is no documented case of a logged dipterocarp forest actually reverting to its original climax state."

The Sarawak forests have existed undisturbed for several million years. They are among the most complex and least studied forests on earth. In the absence of fundamental data on site quality, the growth rates of different tree species, their yields and mortality, their basic biology, and even their taxonomic affiliations, it is difficult to imagine any management strategy being rooted in ecological reality. Sustained yield, an untested hypothesis even in the temperate rainforests, loses all relevance as a scientific concept when applied to an ecological situation whose basic parameters remain essentially unknown.

Page 30 — Dawat Lupung standing by a large tree in the forest

Trees sustain life in all its myriad forms — from the hornbill nesting in the hollow of a trunk to the tiny frogs swimming in a water catchment of an epiphytic plant suspended over a hundred feet above the forest floor. A source of warmth and food, medicine and poison, trees create the air creatures breathe, the clouds that envelope the sun, the shelter that protects the living from a violently blue sky. For Penan, trees represent life itself. For them, the notion of measuring a tree by the value of its raw lumber is incomprehensible. "From the forest," they say, "we get our life."

Far from being "wild nomads moving through a trackless wilderness," the Penan view the forest as a homeland, an intricate and living network of economically and culturally significant places linking past, present, and future generations. Imposed from their imagination and experience is a geography of the spirit that delineates time honoured territories and ancient routes which resonate with the place names of rivers and mountains, caves, boulders, and trees. When Dawat speaks of "the land from which we come since long ago," he, like all Penan, recognizes that he walks literally in the footsteps of his ancestors and that his descendants will one day need to follow in his. A sense of stewardship permeates Penan culture, dictating consistently the manner in which Penan utilize and share their environment.

This Penan notion of stewardship is encapsulated in *molong*, a concept that defines both a conservation ethic and a notion of resource ownership. To *molong* a sago palm is to harvest the trunk with care, insuring that the tree will sucker up from the roots. *Molong* is climbing a tree to gather fruit, rather than cutting it down, harvesting only the largest fronds of the rattan, leaving the smaller shoots so that they may reach proper size in another year. Whenever the Penan *molong* a fruit tree, they place an identifying sign on it, a wooden marker or a cut of a machete. It is a notice of effective ownership and a public statement that the natural product is to be preserved for harvesting at a later time. In this way, through time, the Penan have allocated specific resources — a clump of sago, fruit trees, dart poison trees, rattan stands, fishing sites, medicinal plants — to individual kin groups. The Penan acknowledge these as familial rights that pass down through the generations. In many cases the identifying mark on a particular tree takes the form of two parallel sticks — a sign that acknowledges ownership while inviting the wayfarer to share at the proper time in the bounty of the resource. It is the equivalent of a private property sign that reads 'please share wisely' rather than 'no trespassing.'

Page 33 — Wreathed hornbill, fallen fruits on the forest floor, and Borneo bearded pig

Although the Penan hunt hornbill and monkeys, sambar deer, gibbons, mouse deer, civets, squirrels, and a host of other creatures, their principal source of meat is *babui*, a variety of bearded pig endemic to Borneo. Usually active by night, the omnivorous bearded pig lives on a diet of fallen fruits and seeds, roots, leaves, insects, worms, and other small animals. Variable in colour and characterized by a long muzzle with many bristles, the bearded pig is a formidable adversary, sometimes weighing as much as 250 pounds.

The Penan hunt *babui* with spears and packs of small dogs. Once the animal is cornered and killed, a tumpline and shoulder straps of fibrous bark are passed through the skin and the entire carcass, often twice the weight of a man, is hoisted onto the back and carried to camp. There the animal is butchered, with equal portions being meticulously allotted to each family. The liver is roasted and consumed immediately. Other meat that cannot be eaten fresh, is cubed and carefully smoked. The fat, a valuable item of trade, is rendered by the women and stored in sealed three foot lengths of bamboo.

The significance of *babui* and other wild game in the diet of the Penan and other Dayak peoples of Sarawak is considerable. The International Union for the Conservation of Nature and Natural Resources (IUCN) has estimated that indigenous peoples annually harvest over a million wild pigs, 23,000 sambar deer, and 31,000 barking deer, a total of approximately 18,000 tons of wild meat, valued conservatively at US$80 million. Replacing this protein source with domestic pig or beef would cost the Malaysian society more than US$123 million each year. For the Penan, who have no tradition of animal husbandry, healthy populations of wild prey are critical to the survival of their civilization. The loss of the wild pig, the end of the game, would reduce them to mere shadows of what they now are.

In recent years the dramatic increase in logging activity has, in fact, coincided with a serious reduction in the availability of wild game. A study conducted by the WWF suggests that among indigenous peoples, the annual per capita protein consumption has dropped from 54 to 12 kilograms. A Sarawak government study acknowledges that in recently logged areas there has been a threefold increase in malnutrition among Dayak peoples.

The causes of the decline in pig populations are several. *Babui* normally travel in herds of thirty to forty animals, moving seasonally from one area to another in response to the fruiting cycle of the forest trees. In regions of primary forest, and in years of unusually heavy crops of wild seeds and fruit, migrations of as many as a million wild pigs may roam the land in search of food, crossing broad rivers and climbing entire mountain ranges. After an area is logged, food supply is reduced, as many of the commercially extracted species — meranti, kapur, and others — produce copious amounts of fruit. Smaller pig populations do adapt to secondary growth and survive in fragmented patches of forest. Hunting pressure, however, is severe, uncontrolled, and exasperated by the extensive network of logging roads that dissects the forest. For recreation and to augment their wages by selling meat, employees of the logging companies, travelling by open truck and armed with high powered rifles, shotguns, and searchlights hunt by day and night, often driving local populations of *babui* to extinction.

**Page 34 —
Penan boy eating fruit**

Of an estimated 75,000 edible plants found in nature, only 2,500 have ever been eaten with regularity, a mere 150 enter world commerce, and less than twenty, mostly domesticated cereals stand between human society and starvation. Most of the common foods eaten in North America and Europe were first domesticated by indigenous peoples, and in many instances originated in the tropical rainforest. Indeed, if North Americans had to subsist only on cultivated plants native to the USA and Canada, our diet would consist of pecans, cranberries, Jerusalem artichokes, and maple sugar. If it was not for the extraordinary agricultural contributions of Central and South American Indians, the Swiss would have no chocolate, Hawaii no pineapple, Ireland no potato, Italy no tomato, India no eggplant, North Africa no chili, England no tapioca, and none of us would have vanilla, papaya, or corn. The rainforests of Southeast Asia have given the world sugar cane and, most recently, the kiwi, which contains ten times the vitamin C found in oranges.

The forests of the Penan produce a veritable cornucopia of wild fruits, some of which may be unknown to science. Preliminary ethnobotanical surveys suggest that the Penan regularly eat as many as a hundred different kinds of fruits, including the exceptionally sweet *adui*, shown in the photograph being eaten by the boy from Long Bangan. The Penan commitment to sharing reaches amusing and endearing proportions when it comes to wild fruit. The smallest portion is divided, and one is constantly being passed partially eaten pieces of fruit.

**Page 37 —
Asik Nyelik tapping a tajem tree to extract the poisonous latex**
Asik Nyelik, a nomadic Penan hunter, begins the process of making poison by tapping *tajem*, *Antiaris toxicaria*, a tall forest tree employed throughout much of Southeast Asia as an arrow and dart poison. The active ingredient is an extremely toxic cardiac glycoside called antiarin. Unlike curare, a muscle relaxant from the Amazon that kills by causing suffocation, cardiac glycosides interfere with the normal functioning of the heart, precipitating lethal arrhythmias. Both curare and *tajem* are non-toxic if swallowed. For the poisons to work, they must enter the bloodstream.

To prepare the poison, the Penan first make a v-shaped incision in the bark. The latex, which collects in the length of bamboo, is later placed in a leaf container and slowly heated over fire to evaporate the excess fluid. Once the poison achieves a thick viscous consistency, it may be applied to the darts, which are then carefully dried or, alternatively, poured into leaf molds to harden for later use. Stored in bamboo containers and kept cool, the preparation retains its toxicity for up to a year or more. The process of making the poison is relatively mundane. The realisation, however, that this orally inactive substance, derived from a single tree in a vast forest of thousands of species, can kill when administered intramuscularly, is profound.

The Penan maintain that the strength of the poison varies, both from tree to tree and within a single individual, depending on the time of day and season the latex is gathered. No two trees are equally toxic and the potency of a given preparation must be empirically tested by hunting. Depending on the body weight of the prey, the best poisons take ten to fifteen minutes to kill, though reptiles and fowl, the Penan maintain, are more resistent than mammals. Should the poison prove insufficiently toxic, the Penan will augment the preparation with various admixture plants, fifteen of which have been reported to date.

The exact chemical role of these admixtures is uncertain. They include roots and stems, leaves, rhizomes and bark of plants belonging to unrelated families, only some of which are noted to contain pharmacologically active constituents. In each instance the admixtures are used in very small quantities, generally a millilitre or two of ash or grated fresh material. Some, no doubt, are added for their magical properties. The rhizome of *long*, for example, a terrestial member of the philodendron family, is said to ensure that the animal will not feel the impact of the dart. *Laka* is a parasitic plant, *binah*, *sekaliu*, and *telikut* are trees, *tajem moseng* is a very rare liana, *basong* is a ginger. A small one centimetre piece of the root of the liana, *tuwok*, burnt to ash and added to *tajem*, is said to be particularly toxic.

Scientific understanding of the Penan dart poisons is limited due to the lack of ethnobotanical data, and the guarded nature of the information itself. It may well be that the toxic effects of the principal poison are enhanced by the addition of these subsidiary plants. This is an important feature of many folk preparations around the world and it is due in part to the fact that different chemical compounds in relatively small concentrations may effectively potentiate each other. The result is a powerful synergistic effect, a biochemical version of the whole being greater than the sum of the parts.

Page 38 — Mutang Tuo with medicinal leaf on arm
Mutang Tuo of Long Iman demonstrates how the *nyagung* leaf, after being warmed over fire, is applied directly to a sprained shoulder to reduce pain and swelling. Preliminary ethnobotanical surveys suggest that the Penan employ over fifty medicinal plants which they harvest from the primary forest. Plants are administered as antidotes for food poisoning, contraceptives, clotting agents, general tonics, stimulants, disinfectants, and to set bones, eliminate parasites, treat headache, fever, lacerations, boils, snakebite, toothache, diarrhoea, skin infections, and rashes. There are magical plants employed to dispell evil spirits, stop babies crying, or empower hunting dogs. At least five plants — *buhaw*, *sapungan*, *gatimang*, *bhut*, and *batah* — serve as antidotes to the dart poison. In the absence of a thorough ethnobotanical study complete with taxonomically determined voucher specimens and phytochemical data, however, it is impossible to know which of these plants may be pharmacologically active and which are mere supports for sympathetic magic. The first challenge in assessing the potential of the Penan pharmacopoeia entails understanding the belief system that mediates their use of medicinal plants.

In general, indigenous medicine is based on a thoroughly non-western conception of the etiology of disease in which health is defined as a coherent state of equilibrium between the physical and spiritual components of the individual. Health is wholeness, which in turn is perceived as something holy, and in this regard indigenous perceptions are not far removed from beliefs once held by our society. The words health, whole, and holy have the same root in the Old English word *hal*, meaning sound, healthy, whole.

The maintenance or restoration of this balance is the goal of the indigenous art of healing. In our secular society, by contrast, life and death are defined in strictly clinical terms by physicians, with the fate of the spirit being relegated to the domain of religious specialists who, significantly, have nothing to say about the physical well being of the living. In indigenous societies the physician is also the priest, for the condition of the spirit is as important as — and, in fact, determines — the physical state of the body. Good or bad health results not from the presence or absence of pathogens alone, but from the proper or improper balance of the individual. Sickness is disruption, imbalance, and the manifestation of malevolent forces in the flesh. Health is a state of harmony, and for the indigenous peoples it is something holy.

As a result, indigenous medicine acts on two quite different levels. There is an entire range of ailments that is treated symptomatically much as in our society, with only medicinal plants and folk preparations, many of which are pharmacologically active. Much more serious, however, are the troubles that arise when the harmony of the patient's spiritual being is broken. In this case it is the source of the disorder, not its particular manifestation, that must be treated, and the healer must sail away on the wings of trance to a spiritual realm to work his or her deeds of spiritual rescue. Because disharmony will affect all aspects of an individual's life, problems brought to the healer include both psychological and physical ailments, as well as other troubles such as chronic bad luck in hunting, difficulties in conceiving a child, or perhaps a general sense of lassitude and ill ease attributable to a magical spell or malevolent spirit. Each case is treated as unique. As a form of treatment, indigenous medicine does not ignore the presence of pathogens; it simply notes that the pathogens are present in the environment at all times and asks why certain individuals succumb when they do.

The Penan, like most indigenous peoples, believe that spirits are ultimately responsible for sickness and simple ceremonies, led by spirit mediums known as *dayong*, are held to appease the forces of darkness and exorcise the body of the afflicted. The sources of malevolence and disease are several. *Pennakoh* is a malicious and vengeful spirit that seeks refuge in the trunk of the strangling fig tree. A master of deceit and disguise, *pennakoh* lurks in the form of animals or demons, ready to betray the living. The wrath of other spirits is felt by those who ignore the omen birds or violate taboo by killing trees.

The Penan must be particularly careful in all matters related to the dead. Never will they remain in a camp where death has stalked, nor will they mention the name of a dead person, particularly if he or she has been deceased for less than a year. To do so would be to incur certain misfortune. Hence, the Penan use a complex system of death names to refer to those who have passed away. Some groups of Penan, for example, refer to the dead by adding the prefix *dulit* to the name of the place where the person died. Other Penan refer to the dead as *mukun*, a word that normally means aged and implies weakness and decrepitude. This word is prefixed to a term indicating the relationship of the deceased to the speaker. Thus a person refers to a dead sibling as *mukun padi*. Even a dead child will be referred to by the prefix *mukun*. The naming prohibition extends to animals as well. A live wild pig is called *babui*, but once killed it is referred to as *kan*, which simply means meat.

With a spirit world that is alive, the Penan quest for healing and well being is rooted both in magico-religious beliefs and a perspicacious knowledge of pharmacologically active plants. Understanding their folk medicine and identifying those of their plants that may ultimately serve the needs of all human societies is a complex and time consuming task. Unfortunately, as in the case of indigenous societies throughout the world, the traditional knowledge is being lost at a tremendous rate. Logging activities are destroying the source of the medicines even as the forces of acculturation disrupt the integrity of the belief system itself. Understaffed government clinics and itinerant physicians that make rare and brief appearances in the Penan settlements are no substitute for the ancient system of medicine that is now being lost. When Dawat complains about the government issuing Panadol (a painkiller similar to Tylenol) as the sole treatment for illness, he states, "It is already spoiled. The more we take, the sicker we become." Panadol, of course, does not spoil. What Dawat is saying is that a synthetic drug cannot replace the spirit of the plants, imbued as they are with the power to heal.

Page 41 —
Penan medicines in use

Many Penan medicinal plants have several uses. *Gatimang*, for example, is one of the plants employed as an antidote to the dart poison. The petiole of the same plant is chewed as a treatment for stomachache and indigestion. The peeled inner bark of *gatimang* is said to relieve headache when applied to the forehead. The leaves, heated over a fire, repel mosquitoes and keep bees away during honey gathering.

According to the World Health Organization, approximately 88% of the people in developing countries rely chiefly on traditional medicine for their primary health care needs. This high degree of dependence, together with many thousands of years of experimentation, have yielded numerous plants of true pharmacological worth. Worldwide there are about 121 clinically useful prescription drugs derived from 95 species of higher plants, 47 of which are native to the tropical rainforest. Roughly 40% of these drugs are used in North America. Plant ingredients valued in excess of US$8 billion are included in 25% of all prescriptions dispensed by community pharmacies in the USA and Canada. Of the 3,500 new chemical structures discovered in 1985, 2,619 were isolated from higher plants.

Plants are useful as medicines because they have evolved complex secondary compounds and alkaloids as chemical defenses against insect predation. These defensive chemicals, which in certain plants may comprise 10% of dry weight, interact harmfully with the biochemical apparatus of the insects. The same properties, however, can be exploited by the modern chemist for therapeutic purposes.

Once extracted and identified, a chemical compound derived from a medicinal plant may be utilized in various ways. Plant extracts may be used directly as pharmaceuticals. Alternatively, they may serve as templates for the chemical synthesis of related medicinal compounds. Finally, in many cases the natural product may be used as a tool in the process of drug development and testing. Thus, in seeking new drugs, researchers attempt first to identify any compound that is pharmacologically active. In many instances the difference between a medicine, a poison, and a narcotic is a matter of dosage.

To date, only approximately 5,000 out of an estimated 250,000 to 300,000 higher plants have been studied in detail for their possible medical applications. Knowledge of tropical rainforest plants is especially inadequate. Though 70% of all plants known to have anti-tumour properties have been found in the tropics, over 90% of the Neotropical flora has yet to be subjected to even superficial chemical screening. At least 85% of the world flora of higher plants have yet to be examined for anti-cancer activity. In the Amazon, a mere 470 out of 80,000 species of higher plants have been investigated in detail. Any practical strategy for expanding knowledge of this living pharmaceutical factory must include ethnobotanical work among the indigenous societies who best understand the forest. To attempt to assay the entire flora without the consultation of indigenous people would be logistically impossible, intellectually short sighted, and historically uninformed. Seventy-four percent of the 121 biologically active plant-derived compounds currently in use worldwide were discovered in a folk context, the gifts to the modern world of the shaman and the witch, the healer and the herbalist, the magician and the priest.

Tragically, the rate of destruction of biological and cultural diversity promises to rob us within a single generation of the accumulated wisdom of millennia. The cost of our folly may be measured in dollars. In the USA alone, the value in terms of pharmaceutical potential of one species of higher plant destined to become extinct by the year 2000 has been estimated to be $203 million. Based on this figure, the value of all the plants in the world expected to disappear in the next decade is astronomical.

Page 42 — Rattan gathering, basket weaving and finished basket

The material culture of the Penan, like that of all nomadic peoples, is by necessity rudimentary and what few objects they keep must satisfy all of their basic needs. Their technology, therefore, is simple but elegant and predictably based on the continual exploitation of forest plants. The most important resource is rattan which provides the raw material for baskets, backpacks, mats, wrist and ankles bracelets, roofing, and general tying purposes. The Penan regularly harvest at least twenty-five different species in three genera of rattan palms. The most important is *Calamus*, a genus of spiny climbers with distil leaflets modified as backward pointing spines that act as grapples, allowing the palm to grow up from the forest floor, reaching lengths of 180 meters as it climbs into the canopy. The genera *Korthalsia* and *Daemonorops* are also important rattan sources.

With rattan, Penan women weave intricate and beautifully patterned artifacts that are renowned throughout Sarawak, and much in demand among neighbouring Dayak peoples and itinerant Chinese and Malay traders. The principal woven objects include flat carrying baskets known as *gawang*, round baskets called *bukui*, heavier baskets, or *kivah*, that serve as backpacks, and ornate mats for sleeping called *mak*, or processing sago, known as *tabau*. The baskets generally take two days to a fortnight to complete, the mats anywhere from two weeks to two months.

Other important resources extracted from the primary forest include plants used as vegetable dyes and soap, wood to make musical instruments and for firewood. Their environment provides implements for firemaking — flint, tinder, and *aka korek*, a liana that smolders for days used to transport fire. It also provides all the elements of their hunting and fishing technology — dart and fish toxins, *nyagang* and *pa tanyit*, wood for blowpipes, *jakah*, leaf stalks for making darts, and gums — *makan* and *talum* — employed to capture birds. The forest provides trade items such as *gutta percha*, *damar*, and *garu* wood, construction materials — *kayu kulit* bark used to make walls, bamboo and palm fronds used for roofing, wood employed for building shelters and *laka bakala* used as sandpaper.

Page 45 — View from the mountain of Gunung Api in Gunung Mulu National Park

The trail that rises from the mouth of the Melinau Gorge to the Pinnacles traverses the flank of Gunung Api, affording a breathtaking vista across a vast expanse of lowland mixed dipterocarp forest. Most of the forest seen in this photograph lies outside the boundaries of Gunung Mulu National Park and within the 300,000 acre logging concession of Datuk James Wong, parliamentary representative for the Limbang Division for thirty one years and currently Minister of the Environment and Tourism. Any effort to expand the park or create a Biosphere Reserve around it will inevitably clash with the economic interests of Mr. Wong.

A pioneer in the Sarawak logging industry, Mr. Wong does not believe that his industry is detrimental to the forest. "It is wrong to say that logging causes serious environmental problems," he has said. "It has been proven that logged over areas will return to normal after five years. Shifting agriculture causes more destruction than logging." Most environmental authorities would disagree.

Shifting, also known as slash and burn or swidden agriculture, with its cycle of clearing, burning, and planting, one or two good crop yields followed by seasons of diminishing returns and long periods of regenerative fallow, has long been recognized as the most adaptive means of farming in the lowland tropics. More than any other agricultural system devised by man, shifting cultivation simulates the structure, functional dynamics, and equilibrium of the natural forest. It is the way the settled Dayak peoples have farmed for generations.

Critics of shifting agriculture maintain that the periodic need to cut and burn the forest is inherently wasteful. They measure the lifespan of a field in terms of the principle cultigen — usually rice in Sarawak — and suggest that once it can no longer be productively grown, the field must be abandoned and a new section of primary forest felled. In fact, recent research has shown that the time devoted to the production of the primary crop is but a phase in the organic evolution of the agricultural setting. Long after the two or three peak years of production, the fields continue to yield domestic plant products and a plethora of useful raw materials including medicines, fish poisons, dye plants, insect repellants, body cleansers, firewood, and materials for making thatch, rope, packaging, and crafts.

More importantly, in almost every instance, new swidden fields are cut from secondary growth, not from primary forest. Evidence from throughout Southeast Asia suggests that in most regions the system of shifting agriculture has remained stable for centuries. In Sarawak, a study by Christine Paddoch of the New York Botanical Garden, indicated that the Iban have farmed their areas of settlement for over three hundred years. Contrary to the opinion of Minister of the Environment and Tourism Wong, shifting agriculture is a stable practice dependent not on the progressive destruction of primary forest but on the continual recycling of land first settled generations ago. In 1985 in Sarawak, shifting agriculture destroyed at most 18,000 hectares of primary forest. In the same year industrial logging occurred on 270,000 hectares.

That shifting agriculture as opposed to logging is the main cause of environmental degradation in Sarawak is a notion maintained and promoted by the highest government authorities. Malaysian Prime Minister Datuk Mahathir Mohamad has said, "You are wrong if you think giving the forests to the indigenous peoples will save the trees. The indigenous peoples practise slash and burn cultivation and vast tracts of forest have been completely obliterated by shifting slash and burn practise. Logging of selected mature trees allows the forest to regenerate quickly."

In maintaining that swidden agriculture is more destructive than logging, the government critique shifts responsibility for the current forestry crisis to the indigenous peoples. In *Natives of Sarawak*, Evelyn Hong writes, "Ironically, this attack is lead by planners, policy makers, and bureaucrats who are the very people responsible for the wholesale logging of tropical forests, causing massive erosion, depletion of precious top-soil, ecological disruption, and climatic imbalances in the environment."

Clearly it is logging and not swidden agriculture that poses the immediate threat to Sarawak's primary forests. At present, forested areas completely secured from logging are limited to 251,655 hectares currently preserved in six national parks and two wildlife sanctuaries. Six additional parks totalling 207,730 hectares are in the planning phase. The creation of national parks, however, while securing the biological integrity of some selected areas, has failed to date to address the important issue of indigenous rights and tenure. Gunung Mulu National Park, for example, was created in 1974 without any consultation with the Penan, the traditional inhabitants of the region. Penan families, in fact, have been obliged to leave their traditional land and resettle outside of the park.

Although the government expressly permits the Penan to hunt and gather within the park boundaries, there are numerous reports of harassment. In November 1989,

members of the Endangered Peoples Project witnessed a National Park Officer interrogate and record the names of two Penan who had collected a few medicinal leaves within the park boundary.

A Penan hunter passing through the area with the carcass of a small mouse deer felt compelled to conceal his catch from the same park officer. Interviews conducted in the settlements located along the periphery of the park suggest both that the Penan view the park as an imposition on their traditional land, and that they fear that the government may, in the near future, extinguish their hunting and gathering rights within the park boundary.

Page 46 — Ruan Katan sitting in forest shelter

Ruan Katan, of Long Tikan, rests in a *tapung*, a traditional shelter used by the Penan when they are on the move. This structure, little more than a waterproof lean-to, is readily constructed in less than an hour from forest materials—saplings, split bamboo, rattan, and palm fronds. More elaborate shelters known as *lamin*, each housing a single family, and complete with earthen hearths for cooking, platform sleeping areas for the hunting dogs, slat shelves overhead for storage, and raised floors accessed by notched poles, are built as temporary settlements in areas of abundant food. These settlements serve as base camps, sheltering the young and the elderly as the adults radiate through the forest. Depending on the resource base, the Penan may occupy a settlement for a few weeks or several months.

Major movements generally occur three or four times a year, though a death will invariably precipitate a move, often within a matter of hours of the event.

For the Penan, as for all peoples, death is the first teacher, the first pain, the edge beyond which life as they know it ends and wonder begins. Possessing no digging tools, Penan do not bury their dead. Instead, the bodies are wrapped in mats and laid with a few personal effects on the forest floor, perhaps beside a tree, by a waterfall, between two boulders, or along a stream or some other landmark that the deceased was familiar with in life. Occasionally the dead are placed on platforms to protect them from animals or left in the abandoned *tapung*, or *lamin*, where they died, to await dissolution amidst the decaying ruins of their former shelter. In the aftermath of a death, the survivors move on, threading their way through the forest to another site long visited by their kin group and ready once again to be occupied.

Page 49 — Dawat drinking from Melinau River

Nomadic Penan groups generally include between fifteen and forty people. Though individuals are often widely dispersed in the forest, a most extraordinary dialogue is maintained by means of sign-sticks, branches, or saplings strategically placed and decorated with symbols that convey specific messages. The symbols are not universal, but are understood by members of any particular group. These sign-sticks can indicate where and when a party has split up, the direction each group has travelled, the anticipated length of the journey, the difficulty of the terrain, and whether or not food is available. Some are symbols of welcome, others of warning. Messages can instruct a party to return to base camp or advance in a different direction. A four pronged stick implanted in the ground identifies a burial, three sticks placed vertically as a fan claims ownership, one stick appropriately shaved and broken at the tip indicates that a party intends to return to the spot and requests that all other Penan await its arrival.

One stick observed in the Melinau River drainage had the following configuration and message; A large leaf at the top showed that the stick had been left by the headman. Three small uprooted seedlings indicated that the site had once been occupied by three families. A folded leaf told that the group was hungry, in search of game. Knotted rattan gave the number of days anticipated in the journey and two small sticks equal in length and placed transversely on the sign stick suggested that there was something for all Penan to share. Sticks and shavings at the base identified the group and revealed the direction of the journey.

Penan 50 — Primary forest landscapes

For over a million years all human beings were nomads, wanderers on a pristine earth. Our paleolithic ancestors believed in the power of the animals, accepted the existence of magic, acknowledged the potency of the spirit. Magical and mystical ideas entered the very texture of their thinking. Religion was first nursed by mystery, but it was born of the hunt, from the need on the part of humans to rationalize the fact that to live they had to kill what they most revered, the animals that gave them life. Rich and exceedingly complex hunting myths evolved as a covenant between the animals and humans, a means of eliminating the guilt of the hunt and maintaining a certain essential balance between the consciousness of man and the unreasoning impulses of the natural world.

A mere five thousand years ago the Neolithic revolution and the development of agriculture changed forever the relationship between humans and the earth. The agrarian transformation and the advent of sedentary village life, which led in turn to the first religious hierarchies, meant the death of ancient animistic traditions. As the cult of the seed overthrew the hunt, so the priest displaced the shaman. With religious leaders serving as mere functionaries of established religious theologies, the shaman's poetry, inspired by the songs of ten thousand birds, was turned into prose. A new theme entered history. The separation between man and nature set in motion a savage assault upon the earth by human societies that in time came to pride themselves on their aversion to all forms of myth, magic, and mysticism, cultures that grew to view intimacy with nature as a poetic conceit.

The consequences of this worldview lie all around us. We have contaminated the air, water, and soil, driven wild things to extinction, dammed the rivers, torn down the ancient forests, poisoned the rain, and ripped holes in the heavens.

Who can doubt that we must dream new dreams, find new topographies of the spirit, rediscover the scents and sounds and possibilities of an earth fresh with the promise of life and wisdom? The Penan, by their example, give us a sense of what we all once were. In their memories lie the origin and essence of the entire human race.

Page 51— Complex web of life — caterpillar, moth, and snail on pitcher plant
Invertebrates comprise the vast majority of animal species living on the earth today. There are over 8,800 species of ants alone, and in the Amazon, ants and termites make up a third of the total animal biomass. In Borneo, one entomologist identified some 600 species of butterflies and caterpillars in a single day. An estimated thirty million species of insects live in the tropical forest. Though many of these remain unknown to science, they play a critical role in maintaining the vital nutrient cycles of the ecosystem. Were the insect fauna to disappear or decline precipitously, the physical structure of the forest would degrade, and fish, amphibian, reptile, mammal, and bird populations collapse.

Every thirty minutes, somewhere on earth, a species becomes extinct. What is lost forever is an unique evolutionary possibility, the ever changing product of literally millions of natural permutations that began at the dawn of time. A single bacterium possesses about ten million bits of genetic information, a fungus one billion, an insect from one to ten billion depending on the species. If the information in just one ant were to be translated into a code of English letters and printed in letters of standard size, the string of letters would stretch over a thousand miles. One handful of earth contains information that would just about fill all fifteen editions of the *Encyclopaedia Britannica*. This is the true resonance of nature.

One of the biological wonders of the Penan forest is *Nepenthes*, the carnivorous pitcher plant, three species of which are found in elfin forest on the high exposed ridges of Gunung Mulu National Park. One species, *Nepenthes muluensis*, is found nowhere else on earth. A classic indicator of nitrogen poor soils, these plants obtain nutrients by trapping insects in exquisitely formed pitchers, which are, in fact, modified leaf tips. The pitchers develop as intercalary invaginations below the tip of tendrils, with the lips growing out below them. Insects attracted to the nectar and the brilliant colour of the pitchers work their way down the vessel onto slippery cuticles and then slide into the base where they die and decompose.

The Penan call the pitcher plant *telo medok*, which translates literally as the "dart quiver of the short-tailed monkey." These plants, together with a water filled liana known as *laka bekawit*, are useful sources of drinking water.

Page 52 — Datung Den standing in clearcut

A Penan hunter, Datung Den from Long Sepatai crosses a clearing that was once part of his traditional hunting ground. The temperature difference between where he stands in the open sun and the forest just behind him may be as much as seven degrees Celsius. Through the process of evapotranspiration, each forest tree has the cooling effect of twenty, household air-conditioners. Once the forest canopy is removed, the cool, moist microclime dissipates and the searing sun bakes the soil, killing the understory plants that are so vital to the Penan for medicines and food. Sun tolerant plants quickly invade the clearings, growing into a wretched entanglement of half-hearted trees. Whereas the floor of the primary forest is relatively open and easy to traverse, the dense underbrush of the secondary forest can be virtually impenetrable.

Tropical rainforest once covered 95,232 sq. km. of Sarawak. Approximately 30% (28,217 sq. km.) of this heritage was logged between 1963 and 1985. In 1985 alone, logging occurred on 2700 sq. km., the equivalent of 2.8% of Sarawak's total forested land. At the end of 1984, another 44,101 sq. km., the equivalent of 46% of Sarawak's total forested area, were scheduled to be logged. At current rates of harvest, another 30% of Sarawak's original forests will be cut in the next decade. In the time it takes to read a paragraph of this text, another three hectares will have been cut.

By early 1985, some 5.8 million hectares, representing 60% of Sarawak total forested area, had been licenced for future logging. By the time these concessions are exhausted there will hardly be any primary forest left in Sarawak. Yet, every year new, concessions are granted. In the Fourth Division, 24,579 sq. km. out of a total of 34,017 sq km of forest (72%), had been given out as concessions as of 1984. In the Baram alone, more than thirty logging companies are currently working one million acres of forest on land traditionally belonging to the Kayan, Kenyah, and Penan.

Page 55 — Driven from their homeland by logging, relocated Penan live in squalid government resettlements and drink from polluted waters

Since the time of the British, successive governments in Sarawak have sought to draw the Penan out of the forest, encouraging them to settle along the major rivers, initially to facilitate trade and more recently to exert political control. Relocation invariably places the Penan in direct conflict with the riverine Dayaks, the Kayan, and Kenyah peoples, in particular, who understandably resent the intrusion into what they regard as their traditional territory. The Penan are placed in a quandary. In order to claim their customary and legal rights as a Dayak people under Sarawak law, they must act in a manner that compromises their tradition and inevitably antagonises their neighbours.

For any nomadic people, settlement implies the sacrifice of culture. The core of the relocation effort is an explicit attempt to absorb the Penan into the mainstream of Malaysian society. Prime Minister Datuk Mahathir Mohamad has described this goal directly. "We are asking them to give up their unhealthy living conditions and backwardness for better amenities and a longer and healthier lifestyle." Minister of the Environment and Tourism James Wong has reiterated the government's position. "We don't want," he has said, "them running around like animals. The problem is to settle them down. They have to settle down, otherwise they have no rights." Clearly, nomadic rainforest dwellers do not fit the Malaysian image of a modern, developing nation.

In the last two years, the government has attempted to address the concerns of the Penan by proposing a series of initiatives designed to facilitate assimilation. At great expense, and in part as a public relations ploy, a model longhouse was constructed at Batu Bungan, a settlement adjacent to Gunung Mulu National Park, and similar facilities have been promised for other Penan communities. Other proposals promise to extend medical, educational, and technical services, including agricultural training designed to teach the use of tools, planting and clearing techniques, soil preparation, and methods of preparing foods. To date, however, few of these government programs have reached the Penan settlements. Given that, according to the government's own figures, 22% of the residents of the national capital of Kuala Lumpur live as squatters, one might question whether the government is ultimately capable of delivering on its promise of socio-economic development.

Missing from this equation of material development is any calculation of the emotional, psychological, and spiritual costs inherent in the loss of cultural identity. When

Mr. James Wong states that "no one has the ethical right to deprive the Penan of the right to assimilation into Malaysian society," he ignores the historical fact that the Penan themselves have consistently and deliberately chosen not to compromise their traditions. There has been continuous interaction between the Penan and the outside world since the earliest trading contacts occurred under the British. In recent months, the contemporary Penan Association has made clear its commitment to self-determination. "We are not opposed to all change," Dawat Lupung has said, "but we want to choose development based on our needs. A new longhouse like that of the Kayan is fine. But it is not the house of my father, and if it is meant to replace our forest, it means nothing."

**Page 56 —
Three residents of the resettlement village of
Batu Bungan**

Before the confusion wrought by culture contact and decay, the Penan believed in the power of magic, accepted the existence of spirits, and acknowledged the power of the natural world. Critically, the inevitable cognitive steps that a society takes — and must take — to protect such beliefs from falsification, give rise to a closed circular system of thought wherein no event has a life of its own. Magical and mystical ideas enter the very texture of their thinking. There is no incentive to agnosticism. All their beliefs weave together into a web that is not an external structure in which the believer is trapped, but rather, the very texture of his thoughts. He cannot think that his thoughts are wrong. Even if he were a skeptic, he could express his doubts only in terms of the beliefs shared by his peers.

The nomadic Penan share a set of magical beliefs which form a collective worldview that possesses a certain objectivity and reality that dominates the psychological experience of any one individual. A world of few alternatives makes for an absolute acceptance of established tenets of belief, and those beliefs, in turn, have an absolute and exclusive validity. Within these confines the believer can manoeuver with some intellectual ingenuity, but beyond the limits of belief there is only chaos.

When such an integrated belief system is confronted by a novel ideology whose essence is completely contrary, the collision provokes a tempest of confusion. There is seldom room for compromise. One side must yield. So it is that too often in history, independent cultures — unique ways of life, morally inspired, inherently right, and effortlessly pursued for centuries — have collapsed in a single generation.

Christianity, supported as it was by the political, military, and economic power of the British, began to corrode the lives of the Penan some forty years ago. The first missionaries were converted Kenyah from the Upper Baram who contacted the Penan in the Silat River drainage. By 1955, the first Penan had enrolled in Bible School. By 1958, a school had been established. Its first report noted that a group of forty Penan were learning to sing, but regretted that they persisted in singing the same hymn in forty different tunes. By 1985, thirty years after the first missionary efforts, most of the settled Penan had relinquished their animistic beliefs.

The collapse of their spiritual world reverberated through the lives of those Penan who found themselves in the settlements. Omens and taboos, dismissed by the ignorant as idle superstitions, had in fact been vital signs, symbols that taught one how to live, and without them the social world of the Penan imploded. For a thousand years the spirits forbade the killing of trees. Now, under the new order, this was accepted practice. The Penan found themselves living in houses and sitting in churches constructed of boards sawn from the bodies of their spirits. Christianity instructed new ways of dealing with the dead, by burial in plots of land adjacent to the *lamin* of the living. Thus the impetus that for a thousand generations stimulated the Penan to move was extinguished with a single idea.

Today, even those Penan caught in the web of exotic beliefs are asking new sets of questions. A headman on the upper Silat River who has been a Christian all his life, inquired whether Jesus had been a person or a spirit. Told that Jesus had indeed walked the earth, this man disagreed. "We don't believe it," he said, "We have been looking for him in the forest for a long time, but have been unable to find him. How could such a man, said to be so good and so powerful, allow such terrible things to happen to our forest?"

Page 59 — Log sorting ground on the banks of the Baram River

Until 1945, logging in Sarawak was largely restricted to the swamp forests along the coast. After the war, however, the development of portable and efficient chainsaws, powerful skidders, bulldozers, and trucks opened up the interior for the first time. By 1971,

Sarawak was exporting 4.2 million cubic metres of wood, much of it cut from the upland forests of the hinterland. In 1981, log exports totalled 8.7 million and by 1985 had climbed to 10.6 million cubic metres. The post-war timber boom generated massive fortunes and financed a blistering pace of economic growth, particularly over the past two decades. Between 1976 and 1982 the value of timber exported from Sarawak increased from US$138 million to US$525 million. By 1985, exports had increased to US$615 million. Throughout this period vast sums of money accrued to the government. In 1983, direct revenue through export duties, royalties, and miscellaneous taxes totalled US$155 million, fully 34% of the value of the timber exported.

There is a hidden cost to the boom that rarely figures in economic forecasts. The lumber industry in Sarawak currently employs approximately 57,000 workers, 46,000 of whom are actively involved in logging. Roughly half the workforce is Dayak. The safety record of the industry is appalling. Though less than 5% of the Sarawak workforce is employed in logging, the industry, in 1983, accounted for 67% of all fatal occupational accidents in the state. Over the last 17 years more than a thousand workers have been killed, 94 in 1989 alone. In 1980, one in five workers suffered injury and one in four hundred was killed. On the basis of the injuries reported between 1973 and 1984, it appears that seven lives are lost for every million cubic metres logged in Sarawak. A serious injury occurs for every 7000 cubic metres produced. These figures indicate a rate of accidents twenty-one times higher than what has been reported for the logging industry in Canada. The *New Straits Times* reports that over 20,000 workers have been killed or seriously injured in the last two decades.

In Sarawak, there are no laws requiring companies to meet safety codes, no regulations dictating the use of hardhats and proper footware, no limits placed on the hours a worker may spend in the forest. A Workers Compensation Scheme exists, but payments for the loss of limb or life are set at a maximum of US$7,300.

To date, the Penan are the only tribal people in Sarawak who have not entered the logging workforce. No part of their territory is free of the whine of chainsaws, the roar of bulldozers, and the grinding of log truck gears. They call this cacophony *jaauha lipan*, an expression which translates literally to "loud is the voice of the centipede."

Page 60 —
Long tailed
Macaques

One of the stunning primates of Borneo is the long tailed macaque. Native to Southeast Asia and widely distributed, the monkey is gregarious, generally travelling in groups of twenty or more individuals over a territory of fifty to a hundred hectares. Feeding on ripe fruits and a wide array of insects, the long tailed macaques are active from dawn until dusk, often spending a certain part of the day in low trees and brush where they can be readily observed.

Page 63 —
Fairy bluebird

The tropical rainforests of Southeast Asia support over 20% of all living bird species. These range in form and habit from the wreathed hornbill to the elusive argus pheasant, and the delicate Asian fairy bluebird photographed here. The loss of primary forest habitat endangers this and hundreds of other forest species.

Page 64 —
Borneo Gibbon

The Borneo gibbon is one of many primate species dependent on fruit, young leaves, and small insects found in the canopy of Sarawak's rainforests. Completely arboreal, gibbons are the smallest and most agile of the apes. They travel in small groups, generally a male, female, and several young, and maintain territories of twenty to thirty hectares. Gibbons define their territories by sending out loud, bubbling calls shortly after dawn. As the sun strikes the canopy, a thermal boundary is created between the cool of the forest and the warm air above. Projected along this boundary, the calls of the female gibbons reach far across the forest, carrying more than two kilometres, a distance that would be impossible to attain at any other time of day. Endemic to the island, the Borneo gibbon is found only in tall dipterocarp forest, and as its voice is heard less and less, it has become a symbol of a vanishing homeland.

Page 67 — Rainforest animal diversity

From tree frogs and butterflies to orangutans, there is scarcely an animal in the Sarawak rainforest that is not affected in some way by logging. If current logging practices continue in Sarawak many species will be condemned to extinction. A conservative estimate of the world wide rate of extinction is one thousand species a year, mostly from the destruction of forests and other key habitats in the tropics. Within this decade, the figure is expected to rise to ten thousand species a year, a rate of one species per hour. During the next thirty years, scarcely longer than the time it takes for a single generation of humans to come of age and give birth, fully one million species may disappear. Entire groups of animals that have emerged within the last ten million years — manatees, gorillas, rhinoceros, condors, whales — are already close to the end. This spasm of extinction, precipitated by the folly of one species which is itself entirely dependent on the biosphere, has no precedent in history.

For over three years, the Penan and other Dayak peoples of Sarawak have been on the front lines of defence in the most significant struggle of our era — the effort to preserve biological diversity and the integrity of the world's forests. Every day more than 620 sq. km. of tropical rainforest are destroyed worldwide. Each year an area three times the size of Belgium is laid waste. The industrial economy is, in effect, waging a war against the forests of the planet and, at present, it appears to have the upper hand.

The rainforests of Southeast Asia are particularly imperiled. The primary forests that once blanketed much of Thailand, the Phillippines, Peninsular Malaysia, and Sabah no longer exist. The demise of the rainforests of Burma, Indonesia, and Papua New Guinea is imminent. The rate of cut in Sarawak is the highest the world has ever known. Each day 850 hectares of primary forest are logged and nearly all the remaining forest is scheduled to be cut. If current forestry policies continue, within five to seven years all of Sarawak's primary forest outside of a few protected parks will be gone. The most optimistic forecast, one made by the International Timber Trade Organization (ITTO), concluded that at the existing rate of cut, Sarawak's primary forest will be gone in eleven years.

Page 68 — Log barge loading, buyer selecting logs, and Datuk James Wong, Sarawak's Minister of Tourism and the Environment

The banks of the Baram River in Sarawak's Fourth Division are lined literally for miles with stacked logs awaiting export. Although petroleum accounts for a far larger percentage of Sarawak's export earnings than timber, revenues from the oilfields flow almost entirely to the Federal government in Kuala Lumpur. Control of the forestry sector in Sarawak, by contrast, is held strictly by the State government, as outlined in the terms by which Sarawak joined the Malaysian Federation in 1963. As of 1985, licenced logging concessions in Sarawak totalled 5,752,996 million hectares of which 1,342,826 had been exploited and 4,410,170 were scheduled to be logged.

Sarawak has one of the world's most experienced and well funded forestry departments and on paper, forest policy in Sarawak is impressive. In practice, however, forest management has been subverted to serve the interests of the ruling elite, who have used their control of the licencing of logging concessions as a political tool, a source of personal wealth, and a means of retaining economic and political power. The authority to grant or deny logging concessions lies strictly with the Minister of Forestry. Between 1970 and 1981, and ever since 1985, the highly covetted Forestry portfolio has been retained by the office of the Chief Minister. That the office has been used for political and personal financial gain became evident during the run up to the State elections in April 1987.

At a press conference on April 9, 1987, Chief Minister Datuk Patinggi Hagi Abdul Taib Mahmud announced the freezing of twenty-five timber concessions totalling 1.25 million hectares, all belonging to relatives and friends of the former Chief Minister Tun Abdul Rahman Yakub. Estimates of the value of these holdings ranged from US$9 billion to US$22 billion. In retaliation, Tun Abdul Rahman Yakub revealed to the press the names of politicians, friends, relatives, and associates connected to Datuk Patinggi Abdul Taib Mahmud, who together, controlled 1.6 million hectares of concessions. Ironically, the two antagonists are themselves related, Datuk Taib being the nephew of Tun Rahman. Between them, these two quarrelling factions controlled 2.9 million hectares of logging concessions, a figure that amounts to over half of all logging concessions and a full third of Sarawak's total forested land.

Significantly, those who secure the rights to logging concessions are seldom the parties responsible for the extraction of the timber. The logging itself is done on a contract basis by other companies. Among the beneficiaries of the political patronage of former Chief Minister Tun Abdul Rahman were his eight daughters, each of whom was given a concession. Such revelations make clear that the granting of logging concessions has been, in effect, a means of creating a class of instant millionaires, and in recent years nearly every member of the state assembly has become one. With a resource worth literally billions of dollars, the stakes are high. In a recent election, political parties spent over US$24 million competing for a mere 625,000 votes. The fact that the only car factory ever established in Sarawak produces BMWs is a potent symbol of the economic priorities of the political leadership.

The role of Japan in the Sarawak timber industry is pivotal. Japan depends on Malaysia for 85-90% of its tropical wood imports and fully half of Sarawak's production is siphoned north to Tokyo. Ultimate responsibility for the exploitation of the Borneo rainforest lies far from the shores of Sarawak in the powerful trading houses of Japan. In a 1984 speech on the Sarawak economy quoted in Evelyn Hong's *Natives of Sarawak*, then Malaysian Federal Minister, Leo Moggie, acknowledged that "the marketing of Sarawak timber is still very much controlled by the Japanese trading houses, as Sarawak timber companies are largely dependent on these trading houses for their intricate line of credit." Japanese banks provide the start up loans for local logging companies. Japanese companies and foreign aid supply the bulldozers and heavy equipment necessary to extract the logs. Japanese financial interests provide the insurance and financing for the Japanese ships that clog the South China Sea waiting to load the logs that will be sawn in Japanese mills and dispensed to construction firms often owned by the same concern that first secured the wood in Sarawak. Once sawn in Japan, the wood produced by the oldest and perhaps richest tropical rainforest on earth is used principally for disposable construction forms for pouring concrete and throw-away packing crates.

The Japanese holding companies, sogososhas, wield considerable political influence, forging close links between industrial investments and foreign aid. In 1987, a scandal surfaced in the Japanese Diet when it was revealed that 200 million yen of foreign aid funds had been given to Limbang Trading to build logging roads. C. Itoh, one of Japan's nine giant trading companies, owns a major interest in Limbang Trading, the company founded by Sarawak's Minister of the Environment and Tourism, James Wong. The Sarawak government subsequently informed the Japanese that the aid money was needed to construct a school and for roads to service local communities, the very communities who were facing arrest by blockading the logging road expansion. The school in question turned out to have been constructed twenty years before.

Logging practices in Borneo in the last decade have plundered an extraordinary natural resource. Waste in the industry has been estimated as high as 50%. In December of 1983, Tan Sri Ben Stephens, Director of the Sabah Foundation which owns 36% of Sabah's remaining unlogged commercial forest, noted that for every cubic metre of wood sold, another cubic metre is cut but discarded. Ninety percent of the wood that is exported leaves Sarawak as unprocessed logs, resulting in a significant loss of revenue and employment to the state.

Page 71 — Bulldozer cutting trail through primary forest
Studies conducted by the WWF suggest that selective logging, as practiced in the hill forests of Sarawak, removes approximately 34% of the natural cover, even if only seven trees are cut per hectare. Data published by the FAO indicates that fully half of the residual stands of timber are damaged during the extractive process. Industry advocates, by contrast, maintain that the impact of selective cutting is not detrimental to the long term health of the forest. Minister of the Environment and Tourism, James Wong, has stated, in fact, that logging is "good for the forest." When presented with scientific information suggesting otherwise, Mr. Wong replied, "I will not bow to experts. I am the expert. I was here before the experts were born."

In theory, selective logging has far less environmental impact than the clearcut methods employed in temperate rainforests. In contrast to the graphic scenes of desolation encountered throughout the Pacific Northwest of North America, in particular, logged areas of Sarawak remain green and rapidly flush out with secondary vegetation which creates an illusion of paradise. To understand the true impact of selective logging, however, one must see beyond this veil, and past the vast accumulation of well-intended silvicultural theories that, in effect, mask the difficulty of extracting, in an environmentally sound manner, a few select trees from a given area of tropical rainforest.

In practice, most logging operations in Sarawak occur with little planning and no technical supervision. Decisions on how the trees will be cut and how they reach the specified landing areas, lie strictly with the faller and the operator of the bulldozer or skidder. Working on a contract basis with their wage dependent on their production, these men, often poor, uneducated, far from home fighting off hunger with a chainsaw, place little importance on the environmental implications of their actions. Arriving at a setting, the bulldozer operator establishes a landing and then follows the faller from log to log, skidding them one at a time, expanding his skidtrail as the faller works his way deeper into the cutting block. The faller drops the trees in the direction most convenient to him. To reach them, the bulldozer must work its way throughout the setting, carving long, winding, and even circular tracks into the forest floor. With time at a premium, the bulldozer is constantly on the move, not only hauling logs but moving through the forest locating them. Every activity—turning or lifting the logs to attach the cables, pushing two smaller logs together, manoeuvering the bulldozer into place to begin the haul—results in further damage to the forest.

The cumulative effect of hundreds of bulldozers grinding their way each day through the rainforests of Borneo is one of the most significant environmental problems created by the timber industry. In many parts of Sabah, skidtrails and landings have laid bare over 40% of the forest floor. As logging removes the forest canopy, exposing the soils to rain, the compaction of the ground by the extractive process itself, reduces the capacity of the soil to retain water. The result is a dramatically increased rate of erosion which is further exasperated by the extent and methods of road construction. With the exception of major haul lines, most logging roads are built with the sole purpose of extracting the timber in the most economical and expedient way. Little attention is paid to drainage or grade. Erosion is chronic.

In the course of just a few years, the indigenous peoples of Sarawak have seen their clear streams choked with sediment and logging debris. The federal government's own five year plan states that "soil erosion and siltation have become Sarawak's main water pollution problem." In many parts of the state, rivers are permanently turbid, and the impact on fish populations has been disastrous. Silt interferes with the normal respiration of the gills and reduces visibility, making it difficult, if not impossible, for visual feeding fish to find food.

In disrupting the hydrological cycle, the large scale clearing of forests has caused a dramatic increase in surface run-off and flooding. According to Sahabat Alam (Friends of the Earth) Malaysia, in 1981, floods cost the local Dayak economy over US$4.5 million in damage to crops and livestock alone. The Department of Agriculture in Sarawak has stated publically that improved forestry methods must be implemented if flooding is to be controlled.

Page 72 — Penan in the Ulu Limbang area blockading a logging road

In 1987, Dayak resentment and anger over the impact of logging reached a flash point in the Baram District. After having appealed in vain for over seven years to the government to put an end to the destruction of their traditional homelands, the Penan issued on February 13, 1987, a firm and eloquent declaration of their intentions:

"We, the Penan people of the Tutoh, Limbang, and Patah Rivers regions, declare: Stop destroying the forest or we will be forced to protect it. The forest is our livelihood. We have lived here before any of you outsiders came. We fished in clean rivers and hunted in the jungle. We made our sago meat and ate the fruit of trees. Our life was not easy but we lived it contentedly. Now the logging companies turn rivers to muddy streams and the jungle into devastation. Fish cannot survive in dirty rivers and wild animals will not live in devastated forest. You took advantage of our trusting nature and cheated us into unfair deals. By your doings you take away our livelihood and threaten our very lives. You make our people discontent. We want our ancestral land, the land we live off, back. We can use it in a wiser way. When you come to us, come as guests with respect."

"We, the representatives of the Penan people, urge you: Stop the destruction now. Stop all logging activities in the Limbang, Tutoh, and Patah. Give back to us what is properly ours. Save our lives, have respect for our culture. If you decide not to heed our request, we will protect our livelihood. We are a peace-loving people, but when our very lives are in danger, we will fight back. This is our message."

When this proclamation, like all the scores of letters, appeals, and petitions sent by Dayak peoples to state and regional authorities, was ignored, the Penan took direct action. On March 31, 1987, armed with their blowpipes, they erected the first of a series of blockades across a logging road in the Tutoh River basin. In April, a hundred Kayan at Uma Bawang blockaded a road that pieced their territory. In every instance, the actual barriers were flimsy, a few forest saplings bound with rattan. Their strength lay in the people that stood behind them. These human barricades, made up of men, women, and children, the old and the young, began as a quixotic gesture, a mere embarrassment to the government, but soon grew into a potent symbol of courage and resolve. Within eight weeks of the initial blockade, operations in sixteen logging camps had been brought to a halt, at a cost to the timber industry of several million dollars.

Resistance to the logging spread. By October, 1987, Penan, Kayan, and Kelabit communities had shut down roads at twenty-three different sites in the Baram and Limbang Districts. In all, some 2,500 Penan, from twenty-six settlements took part in the protest. For eight months, despite considerable hardship — hunger, heat exhaustion, and harassment by the logging interests — the indigenous peoples maintained their defiant, yet peaceful, blockades, disrupting the logging industry and frustrating state and federal authorities. The dramatic action electrified the environmental movement both in Malaysia and abroad and drew worldwide support. Press coverage in Australia, Europe, and the United States stimulated concern which grew steadily into a sustained international campaign of protest. The Malaysian and Sarawak governments responded defensively, imposing severe restrictions on the media. Military and security forces were brought into play, and police joined the logging companies to assist in the dismantling of the blockades.

In October, 1987, Malaysian Prime Minister, Mahlathir Mohamad, citing a wave of ethnic unrest that threatened political instability, invoked the Internal Security Act of 1960 to suspend the rights and incarcerate ninety-one critics of his regime. Among those detained was Harrison Ngau of Sahabat Alam (Friends of the Earth) Malaysia, a Kayan environmentalist and the most vocal supporter of the Dayak resistance. At the same time, forty-two Kayan natives of the village of Uma Bawang were arrested. Charged on three counts under the Penal Code, they were accused of obstructing the police, wrongful restraint, and unlawful occupation of State Lands. The last charge, in particular, was received bitterly by the people of Uma Bawang, since they had established a blockade on their own land to protect their legally recognized customary rights.

While the dramatic police action temporarily put an end to the blockades, it also precipitated a legal battle which exposed both an inherent contradiction in the government's position and the essential illegality of the logging itself. According to Sarawak Land Code, native customary rights are inviolable. Since logging concessions had been granted by the state authorities without a clear demarcation of customary lands, the land rights of thousands of Dayak peoples had, by definition, been compromised and would continue to be violated as long as logging continued. On July 26, 1987, a Kayan, charged with obstructing a public thoroughfare, was acquitted when the magistrate concluded that the man had blocked a road that was part of customary land and thus had acted in a legitimate and legal defense of his customary rights.

To deflect the entire issue of customary rights, and to protect the logging industry, the State government took legislative action. In November, 1987, it added to the Forest Ordinance amendment S90B, a specific provision that made it an offense for any person to obstruct the flow of traffic along any logging road. The law also permitted forestry officials to enlist the assistance of the agents of the logging concessionaire in the dismantling of any barrier or human obstruction. Penalties for violating amendment S90B include two years imprisonment and a fine of over US$2,000.

With this deterrent in place, the government believed that the blockades would never again disrupt the flow of timber. They were wrong. The injustice of amendment S90B was obvious to the Dayaks. Lolee Mirai, Penan headman, of Long Leng, spoke of the purpose of the amendment: "We, who have rights to the land were, instead, arrested and not the timber companies who have caused damages to our land and properties. The law protects only the companies and causes us to suffer more. The law is not good. It unjustly allows outsiders and the logging companies to come and damage our land."

In May, 1988, the blockades went up again, near Long Napir, bringing to a halt the logging operations of Minister of the Environment and Tourism, James Wong. Two more blockades sprang up in the Upper Baram in September, and four more in October, as the indigenous peoples of the Upper Limbang and Lawas areas joined the protest. Between November, 1988, and January, 1989, blockades occurred at seven sites, and the Sarawak Forestry Department arrested 128 Dayaks, mostly Penan. Many were held for a fortnight and then released. Some, unable to raise bail, were retained for a month.

By the middle of 1989, it appeared as if the government legislation, the repeated arrests, and the long and expensive trials, had broken the resistance of the Dayak peoples. After January, 1989, sporadic blockades, mounted by the Iban in Bintulu and the Penan in Baram, were quickly dismantled by the government. Then, on September 10, 1989, in a massive show of opposition, indigenous peoples in nineteen communities in the Upper Limbang and Baram, erected twelve new barricades. Five days later, the action spread south into the Belaga area. On October 5th, eleven Iban longhouse communities blockaded roads in the Bintulu District. By the end of the fall of 1989, an estimated 4,000

Dayaks had joined the protest, successfully shutting down logging in nearly half of Sarawak.

With pressure mounting, logging companies took the law into their own hands. Importing Chinese vigilantes from the city of Sibu, agents of the industry attempted to intimidate the indigenous peoples. Identity cards were confiscated, blowpipes and dart quivers thrown into rivers, individuals threatened, and, in certain instances, physically beaten. A Japanese manager for a lumber company told the Penan at Long Napir: "If you don't have any food we'll provide it. But if you want compensation, I'll take your heads back to Japan. You have no right to demand anything in regard to the forest. From here to Batu Lawi, all the land is mine."

Sarawak officials did nothing to protect the indigenous peoples from harassment. To the contrary, in the wake of further protests, the government arrested another 117 Dayaks and subjected them to further human rights abuses. Handcuffed behind their backs for the river journey to Miri from the upper Baram, Penan were compelled to urinate and defecate on themselves, all the while being ridiculed as animals by their guards. Once in Miri, eighty-six Penan men were held for two months in Lambir Prison, with inadequate food and water, in overcrowded cells infested with mosquitos. Several had to be evacuated to the local hospital. All suffered physical deprivation and psychological trauma, due not only to their confinement, but also because they knew that in their absence their families would be without food. Finally, on November 20, 1989, following an appeal to the Chief Justice, they were released. It had been the largest number of arrests to date and the longest period of incarceration. The government appeared determined to break the spirit of the Dayak resistance with increasingly harsh and punitive measures.

Page 75 — Penan forging iron spear point, trade goods acquired by the Penan in the days of the White Rajah, and unfolded cawat

The Penan are not inflexible or incapable of choosing their own destiny. The formation of the Penan Association, and its recent political activities, suggest that the Penan fully recognize that change is inevitable and that some accommodation with the outside world is the only way for their civilization to endure. Acquiring the material benefits of the modern world need not, in and of itself, compromise the integrity of the Penan way of life. Throughout history, societies that survive are those fluid enough to adjust to new conditions, new possibilities, and new dreams. This is something the Penan have always known.

The dexterity and ease with which the Penan convert raw steel into exquisite blades is a potent symbol of the culture's ability to incorporate on its own terms elements of the outside world. The photo at left depicts a man from Long Bi, on the Silat River, masterfully working iron to form machetes, or *parangs*, and knives. Obtaining steel bars by trade, the Penan construct simple, but effective, forges with bellows made of bamboo tubes, and a clever pumping mechanism that directs blasts of air across burning coals, readily generating temperatures that allow for the reworking of steel. Hammering red hot steel into finely formed blades, the Penan create *parangs* noted for their excellence and eagerly sought by neighbouring groups. The *parang* is the basic tool used for harvesting, gathering firewood, clearing brush, and building shelters. The *anak parang*, a smaller knife, is carried with the *parang* in a double wooden sheath and used mainly for cutting meat and forest produce.

During the era of the White Rajah, the Penan maintained constant contact with the British through a supervised system of exchange known as *tamu*. Once every two or three months, temporary trading posts were established in the hinterland at the confluence of major rivers. At these open-air markets, the Penan acquired a variety of items including cloth, metal, salt, tobacco, fire arms, ammunition, and cooking pots, in exchange for their fine rattan mats and baskets, and their harvests of hornbill ivory, resins, gums, camphor, damar, bezoar stones, and fragrant medicinal woods such as *gahuru*. Under *tamu*, government officials regulated the trade and guaranteed fair prices for the Penan goods.

Today, *tamu* is no longer practiced and in the nomadic camps, only vestiges remain, old British hunting rifles and fire blackened cooking pots, symbols of a distant era that, for the Penan, has drifted from history into the realm of myth. To them, *tamu* represents a period of their past when they were able to interact freely with the outside world, taking from it what they chose and discarding what had no place in their culture. It was a time when their right to exist as a people was recognized and acknowledged by law and practice, when they had their land, were free to initiate contact on their own terms, and had time to adjust to the world around them.

Page 76 — Penan children in recently built government resettlement longhouse at Long Sepatai

Long Sepatai, a Penan resettlement camp on a remote tributary of the Abang River, was particularly affected by the long imprisonment of the Penan men in the fall of 1989. With virtually all their hunters in jail or otherwise engaged in political activity and absent from the village, the children, women, and elderly faced hunger and, in certain instances, starvation. Other Penan settlements also suffered immense deprivation. Wan Malong, headman of Long Latik, noted in testimony recorded at a January 20, 1990 meeting of the Penan Association: "My grandfather died as a result of lack of food in September, 1989, when he could not get any meat to eat. If the companies' activities continue, more Penan will die as a result of diseases and lack of food."

At the heart of government resettlement efforts are two critical themes. First, the government expressly seeks to assimilate the Penan and all other Dayaks into the main-stream of Malaysian society. Whether this should occur and just what it entails are not at issue. The only question raised by government planners is how soon this amorphous goal may be achieved. In a speech given at the opening of a tourist centre designed to display Sarawak's cultural diversity, and constructed adjacent to the Holiday Inn Damai beach resort, Chief Minister Tan Sri Taib stated, "There is a big sociological question as to how fast they (the Penan) can be brought into the mainstream of development. But our answer is that there is nothing better than trying." At the January 20, 1990 meeting of the Penan Association, Ajang Kiew from Long Beluk referred to the essence of this development effort. "We ask for schools," he said, "the government brings tractors. We ask for clinics, they give lorries to bring more logs from the area."

The second theme revealed by all the actions and initiatives of the government concerns the way that land and wealth shall be distributed in Sarawak. No amount of bureaucratic jargon can conceal the fact that the resettlement and assimilation of the Penan and other Dayak peoples frees the government to exploit the land as it sees fit. The wealth generated by the forests benefits a small economic and political elite that lives in considerable luxury in Kuching. Chief Minister Tan Sri Taib, for example, lives in a well-guarded palatial home, rides in a cream coloured Rolls-Royce, and wears a ring with a walnut-sized red gemstone surrounded by small diamonds. Such ostentatious displays of wealth stand in marked contrast to the situation of the rural poor. A study conducted by the Flying Doctor Service (FDS) in the hinterland of Sarawak reported that nearly one-third of the infants (27.2%), almost half of the toddlers (46.9%), and three-quarters (74.6%) of the preschool children suffer malnutrition.

In a report published in the Asian Wall Street Journal (February 7, 1990), journalist Raphael Pura revealed that the sixteen logging concessions in the upper Baram are held by just four ethnic Chinese timber groups. Outside of expenditures on salaries and local services, the logging activity generates little revenue for the local communities. According to Pura's report, Rimbunan Hijan, a logging concern owned by the Tiong family, took in approximately US$770 million in revenue between 1976 and 1987. The audited financial statements of the company show that it made a cumulative profit of just US$1.23 million during that period. Records show that Rimbunan Hijan paid its directors and shareholders almost as much in fees and dividends as it paid the Federal Government in taxes.

Page 79 — Penan elder, woman surrounded by children, and three young boys in the forest

In the past, when confronted by aggression, the Penan simply fled into their forests. A peaceful people, they are the only indigenous people in Borneo with no history of headhunting. In their language, there is no expression for "thief," only the word *ava*, which designates one who takes another's head. Thievery, like headhunting, was an exotic act unknown to the Penan. Today, when confronted by an assault on their way of life unprecedented in their history, their language fails them. Dawat's understated comment, "That's what we don't like," seems to be their ultimate expression of anger. There are no words in the Penan language for warfare or aggression. Thus their language of protest has a muted eloquence that merely hints at the depths of the injustice and misery of their situation.

Along Sega, headman of one of the last nomadic bands of Penan, speaks for all of his people:

"When the loggers first came into our land, they said, 'We are going to make a reserve for you. We are only passing through this area and getting logs somewhere else." When we were away, they came and destroyed our land and bulldozed the areas where we bury our dead and collect rattan and poison for poison darts. All the products of the jungle like rattan, animals, fish, and many other things—this is what our life depends on. They are gone."

"The environment minister said we don't have to worry about our land being destroyed because whatever we want, even money, will be given to us. I said, 'I am not going to take any money from you. Your eyes may fall out of your head to see how much money you have, but I am not going to take any of it.' "

"We are stubborn because we have been living in this area for so long, and our heart tells us that this is our land. We are not afraid of going to jail because we know that if the logging continues, we are going to die anyway. Tell the timber companies to stop. This is what we want. Only then will we be happy."

"Even though we are angry and we say these harsh words, we are like animals that have no teeth. We are like an animal that has no claws. If they continue to extract timber from our forest, our lives will wither like leaves on the trees, like fish without water."

Page 80 — Asik Nyelik in a rice field near Long Iman

In a field of rice that grows where the forest once stood, Asik Nyelik, headman of Sungai Ubong, contemplates the life and death struggle of his people. The

government of Sarawak insists that the settled way of life holds the only possible hope for the Penan. It does little, however, to ease the transition, the suffering, and poverty created by forestry policies that place profits above people and the land itself. Asik was not born to labour under the harsh sun, clearing the forest, sowing seed, only to sit in a tin-roofed hovel awaiting a harvest of despair and lost desire.

In an interview recorded in the Marudi office of Sahabat Alam (Friends of the Earth) Malaysia, Asik Nyelik had this to say:

"Long ago, we Penan lived in stone caves. We did not know how to build *sulaps* at that time. We make fire from stone and our *chawat* was made from the bark of trees. We hunt animals. We sharpened stones to cut the meat. We did not have metal knives or spears. To catch fish, we used *beluruk* made from fronds of palm trees. Sometimes we used the bark of trees, or their fruits, to poison the fish to catch them."

"My people have lived in Sungai Ubong since the days of Tamen Tering, who later was succeeded by Tamen Laje, who was succeeded by Paren Kusin, who was succeeded by Dulit Lesu, who was succeeded by me. There were other headmen before Tamen Tering, but now they are gone."

"Sungai Ubong is our home. Our ancestors have chosen this place as their home. They were born and they have lived, died, and were buried here. They also told us where the sago palms were found. They showed us where to look for the fruit trees. They have asked us to look after the land and to take care of the palms and fruits so that future generations have land to live in and food to survive on. And, likewise, I have told my children the same thing. Even now, you can ask my children; they can tell you where to find all the palm and fruit trees."

"In the jungle, everything is there since the days of our ancestors. If our sago flour finish, we would go to the *palo*, the palm trees. If we want to eat fruits, we go to look for the fruit trees. And if we want to eat fish, we set up our *beluruk* to catch them. The animals are there for us to hunt for meat."

"Sago is our food and there are plenty to be found on our land. We Penans of Sungai Ubong do not eat rice, so why do we need to farm? People in town eat roti like their ancestors, so they must farm. They have to rear pigs, chickens, or else buy them because there are no more animals to hunt in their land, or fish to catch in their rivers, as all of these have died or run away due to the destruction. This is why we Penan do not want our land and forest destroyed."

"Our land guarantees our survival. Food is plenty and free here. When we need something, like clothes or knives, we collect some rattan or other forest produce to sell or exchange. Our ancestors have always done this. And in the days of the British when they go for the *tamu*. So, since the time of our ancestors, we Penan have had everything we need. Why should we go elsewhere? The bodies of our ancestors are buried in Sungai Ubong so why should we leave them?"

"All we Penan know is that we human beings cannot create land, only God can. If our land in Sungai Ubong belongs to somebody else, we want to ask them, 'When did you create the land, or plant the fruit trees there, and where are the burial grounds or *sulaps* of your ancestors there?' "

Page 83 — Penan father with his sick child at Batu Bungan

Perhaps the most tragic consequence of the re-settlement of the nomadic Penan has been the marked increase in the incidence and seriousness of disease. A nomadic people, accustomed to moving through the forest in small groups, now find themselves in squalid camps, living in crowded facilities lacking any semblance of proper sanitation. The predictable result is a dramatic increase in morbidity due, in particular, to parasitic infections, dysentery, tuberculosis, conjunctivitis, and rheumatic fever. In many settlements, virtually every child is afflicted with skin diseases such as impetigo and scabies. Fungal and staphylococcus infections, nurtured, in part, by the humid conditions inside the tin-roofed longhouses, are rampant. With incomplete immunization of children, diseases such as measles, mumps, rubella, and diphtheria are not uncommon.

The susceptibility of the Penan to all forms of disease is increased due to the deterioration of the nutritional state of those living in the settlements. An estimated 20% to 50% of the children suffer some form of malnutrition. Deficiency in Vitamin A has led to cases of keratomalacia, an eye disorder unknown in populations of nomadic Penan. In addition, the fly-in doctor service, much touted by the Sarawak government, is seriously substandard. Monthly visits by helicopter (when and if weather and funding permits), bring a doctor to dispense pain killers such as Panadol. Thus, cut off from the forest that once supplied hundreds of medicinal plants, and inadequately serviced by the medical authorities of the state, the Penan living in the settlements find themselves caught in a vicious cycle of malnutrition and disease unlike anything known to their ancestors.

Page 84 — Primary forest after a rain shower

When Dawat asks for help in saving some part of the Penan forest homeland, he asks rhetorically, "Up to how many acres? Up to how many acres?" In truth, despite several decades of scientific research, no one yet knows how large a preserve must be in order to protect a topical forest ecosystem. It's known, however, that the more complex the ecosystem is, the larger the protected area must be. Decreasing the boundaries of a proposed preserve increases the number of species excluded from the net of protection.

But Dawat's question is really metaphorical. How much, he asks, is it worth to have some vision of a world untrampled by greed, where the wild things have a place to rest? How long will it take for people to realise that every forest represents the genetic endowment of eons, that every time a culture disappears, a view of the world becomes extinct? How long will it take for people to understand the beauty and significance of diversity?

The fate of the Penan and their forest homeland have become an international symbol of hope. In the face of overwhelming odds, and at great personal sacrifice and suffering, they have confronted, with dignity and poise, immense and violent forces of opposition.

Their struggle has laid down a challenge to the entire world. Here is a relatively small area of tropical rainforest, universally recognized for its biological significance. It is found in a prosperous nation, blessed with abundant natural resources and unsaddled by debt or population pressures. If a means cannot be found to protect this land, if the ravages of logging are permitted to sweep clean this forest and the remarkably peaceful human beings who know it best, then what chances do we have to resurrect the spirit of our race in more troubled parts of the earth?

Page 87 — Penan boys at Long Sepatai

Increasingly, after years of futile lobbying and peaceful protest, the Penan look to the outside world for support. Just before the September 1989 blockades began, eighty indigenous leaders signed a joint statement intended for global dissemination: "We ask for help from people all over the world. We are people with a proud culture and way of life that is built on our forest and land. Don't take our forest and culture and dignity away. We thank everyone who thinks of us and helps us, even though you are so far away. It is knowing this that keeps us alive."

Without continued international pressure, it is highly unlikely that the Sarawak government will recognize the rights of the Penan, or take action to protect their forest homeland. Vested interests have indicated that they intend to maintain the forests of Sarawak as the exclusive preserve of the State, the domain of the political elite and those who profit by their association with it. These same authorities have made it clear that they will tolerate no opposition to their policies. The strong arm of the law has become increasingly less tolerant, and encounters with the police more brutal with every new blockade. It is imperative that the global community respond to this situation.

Kurau Kusin, headman from Long Kidah, refers to the land as a womb of the people: "It is our birthplace, and it is the resting place of our dead. They have passed the land and forest in their natural state to us so that we can get our food in abundance and need not go elsewhere." What the Penan say of their forest homeland, we ourselves must say of the entire earth. It is our birthplace; it is our only home. We need our wildlands, alive and intact, because they stand apart as symbols of the naked geography of hope.

Back Cover — Penan men crossing the Abang River

Page 88 — Dawat

After Dawat had finished speaking, there was silence. Only the forest sounds of distant birds and cicadas remained.

Photo Credits

All photos by **Thom Henley** except:

page 13; page 33 bottom left; page 42 bottom left; page 55 bottom left; page 56, page 64; page 68 top right, bottom right and page 79 left — **John Werner**

page 9; page 37; page 50 left; 55 top left; 79 bottom right and page 80 — **Wade Davis**

page 71 — **Ken Lay**

front and back inside dust jacket — **Jeff Gibbs**

page 75 left — **Tim Matheson**

page 72 — **Unknown**

Back cover — **Ron Aspinall**

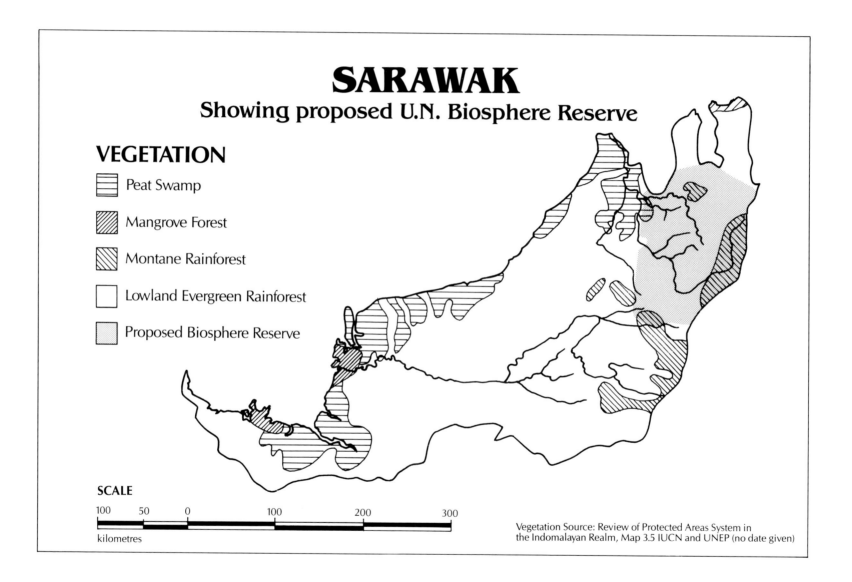

SARAWAK
Showing proposed U.N. Biosphere Reserve

VEGETATION

- Peat Swamp
- Mangrove Forest
- Montane Rainforest
- Lowland Evergreen Rainforest
- Proposed Biosphere Reserve

SCALE

100   50   0   100   200   300

kilometres

Vegetation Source: Review of Protected Areas System in
the Indomalayan Realm, Map 3.5 IUCN and UNEP (no date given)

The Real Work

Wade Davis

In British Columbia, some 950 miles north of Vancouver and 150 miles inland from the richest temperate rainforest on earth, I operate a modest fishing lodge on a remote alpine lake. Yesterday, as I was renovating one of the small cabins, my thoughts passed unexpectedly to the Penan. The previous owner had lined the cabin walls with cheap veneer board made out of thin wooden plys turned from hardwood logs glued together with a photo-imprint giving the false look of knotty pine on the outside. When I ripped one of these sheets from a wall, I noted that it had been manufactured in Taiwan. That meant almost certainly that the wood had originated in the tropical rainforests of Southeast Asia. Since Taiwan imports a large percentage of its wood from Sarawak, it was entirely plausible that this unattractive sheet of veneer had been produced from a tree that once graced the homeland of the Penan. It struck me as a haunting possibility. Here, in the land of red cedar and Douglas fir, where the best of our own timber is shipped overseas, we build with wood ripped from the forests of Southeast Asia and transformed, by some technological sleight of hand, into a parody of our own lumber that we can no longer afford to buy.

This is the first lesson of tropical rainforest conservation. One way or another, we are all involved. Each time we drive to the local supermarket, we ride on tires of rubber produced on plantations carved from the Malaysian forest, and in doing so we burn up a share of the world's finite inventory of oil, a great deal of which is pumped from beneath the coastal waters or the tropical forests of Ecuador, Colombia, Venezuela, Nigeria, Peru, Malaysia, and Indonesia. Each time we buy tropical fruits or oils, consume cola based drinks, chocolate, sugar, imported beef, illicit drugs such as cocaine, and a host of other products, we are participants in an economy based directly on the transformation of tropical rainforests. Furniture and cabinets carved from exotic hardwoods, picture frames, kitchenware, boat decking, interior finishings — all are elements of a cycle of consumption impacting upon some area of the tropics.

In accepting responsibility for our role in the destruction of tropical rainforests, we also empower ourselves with the right and obligation to act, not only to change our patterns of consumption, but also to protect the forests themselves, in whatever region of the earth they flourish. To speak out in defense of the tropical rainforests, however, is a delicate exercise fraught with complexity and inherent contradiction, particularly for those of us nurtured on European, Australian, or North American wealth. Third world politicians who support current development practices suggest, accurately, that the prosperity of North America, in particular, was secured in part by the eradication of the primary temperate hardwood forests of the east, the complete destruction of the tall grass prairie, and the ongoing decimation of the temperate rainforest of the Pacific Northwest. They note that the average North American family's consumption has forty times the environmental impact of the average East Indian family and a hundred times that of the average Kenyan family. The USA has 5% of the world's population and produces 15% of the world's acid rain, and 25% of the industrially produced carbon dioxide and nitrogen oxides emissions. Paper consumption in undeveloped countries averages 15 lbs./person/yr. while in North America it is 650 lbs./person/year. The proponents for development living in the Third World, noting these statistics, rhetorically ask, what are we going to do about this?

The answer is, plenty. We who call for the protection of the Penan homeland are equally vocal in the defense of biological and cultural diversity in North America, Europe, and Australia. Secondly, we recognise that protection has a cost and that this economic burden must be shared multilaterally by both the international community and the host nation. Debt equity, debt for nature swaps, and debt for indigenous stewardship exchanges are but three mechanisms that address this issue directly. Thirdly, we acknowledge that the need for conservation must be balanced with the social and economic requirements of people. No protected area will endure if it conflicts with a people's fundamental struggle to survive. Issues of social justice, sustainable development, and equitable income distribution are, in fact, at the heart of the international critique of Malaysian environmental policy.

What we refuse to accept, however, is the legitimacy of economic arguments that exploit the issue of jobs and national sovereignty as a means of rationalising forest destruction. The argument that would value short term employment over the long term integrity of the ecosystem upon which that employment depends is as valid for the penultimate tree as it is for a living forest. Therefore, somewhere a line must be drawn. When the wealth of the forest demonstrably benefits only a small economic and political elite, and when the forest resource is being cut at a rate that ensures the demise of the industry, the jobs issue is exposed as a chimera.

The concept of national sovereignty, invoked as a means of abdicating ecological responsibility, is equally transparent. In many instances Third World countries, including Malaysia, reflect historical and geopolitical arrangements forged within the last decades from the residue of colonial empires. Malaysia is not yet thirty years old and this time span does not, in any moral or ethical sense, grant it the right to abuse, in the name of national sovereignty, a

resource of global significance. This, at least, is the opinion of the ancient indigenous nations — Penan, Iban, Kenyah, Kelabit, Kayan and others who now find themselves beneath the umbrella of the Malaysian Federation.

What we seek is preservation, not of all the remaining primary tropical rainforests of the earth, but of the absolute minimum 10-20% deemed necessary to ensure the survival of all the world's natural rainforest habitats. To date, only 3% of the rainforest in Africa, 2% in Southeast Asia, and 1% in Central and South America, has come under meaningful protection. The fate of the unprotected forests will be determined within the next two decades. There is tremendous progress yet to be made. Still, the last fifteen years have witnessed extraordinary environmental victories.

Responding to public pressure, Burger King cancelled US$35 million in rainforest beef contracts, Scott Paper Company cancelled US$700 million in pulp mill projects, and the World Bank has withdrawn hundreds of millions of dollars that were designated for dam construction that would have destroyed primary rainforests. National parks and wildlife preserves now protect 200,000 sq. km. of tropical forest. Sixty-five countries support 250 Biosphere Reserves, a quarter of which protect tropical rainforest.

Within the last two years, Colombia and Guatemala have set aside millions of acres of forest in the northwest Amazon and Peten jungles respectively. The recently created Maya Biosphere Reserve in Guatemala, one of the poorest countries of the Western Hemisphere, embraces 1.4 million hectares, a full third of the Peten, which is itself a third of the national territory. It is expected to generate US$60 million a year in tourist revenue and a further US$28 million due to the extraction of renewable natural products from the living forest. Most importantly, it protects a world heritage biological and cultural treasure.

These historic actions taken by both Colombia and Guatemala in defense of their nation's ecological heritage are elements of a geography of hope that is sweeping the world. In a time of shifting political alliances and democratic transformations, the environment is emerging as the central metaphor that links the destiny of all peoples and nations. Within the last three years, environmental awareness and international concern for the fate of the world's rainforests has brought together an extraordinary coalescence of forces destined to secure the integrity of the Sarawak forests and the rights of the Dayak peoples.

It began, appropriately, within Sarawak with the defiance of the Dayak peoples themselves, whose actions on the barricades captivated the international environmental community. The Dayak cause was taken up in Malaysia by Sahabat Alam Malaysia (SAM) — the national affiliate of Friends of the Earth. For several years, members of SAM, led by S.M. Mohd Idris and represented in Sarawak by Harrison Ngau, had championed indigenous rights and rainforest preservation and called for a moratorium on all logging activities in Sarawak. In 1987, Harrison Ngau was arrested and detained under the Internal Security Act. This flagrant abuse of justice drew international attention not only to the victim but to the cause he championed. In 1988, SAM was one of three recipients of the Right Livelihood Award, the alternative Nobel Prize. In 1990, Harrison Ngau received the prestigious Goldman Award for risking his own well being for the sake of the rainforests.

In 1988, international concern became manifest in a series of dramatic developments. In July of that year, a motion was placed before the European Parliament calling for all member nations to ban timber imports from Sarawak until it could be demonstrated that the industry was not detrimental to the biological and cultural integrity of the region. The import ban did not pass, but it came close enough to stun Malaysian officials. In Australia, meanwhile, dock workers threatened to refuse to unload timber imported from Malaysia. In Japan, Japan Tropical Forest Action Network (JATAN) called for a boycott of all tropical hardwoods, a strategy that was later taken up by the Rainforest Action Network (RAN) in both the USA and Australia. In Britain, several large furniture makers announced that they would no longer use certain tropical woods. In the Netherlands, municipal councils refused to grant building permits to construction projects that specified the use of tropical timber. In November of 1989, a second motion came before the European Parliament calling for the release of all detainees in Sarawak, and the resolution of the conflict in a manner satisfactory to the indigenous peoples. This time the motion passed unanimously.

Support for the protection of the Sarawak forests grew as media attention and the broadcast of British and Australian documentaries, in particular, prompted spontaneous actions by concerned parties throughout the world. Individuals wrote letters, circulated petitions, and organized boycotts and demonstrations. Organizations such as Survival International, Friends of the Earth, Amnesty International, and Cultural Survival disseminated the latest information, much of it coming from field research conducted in Sarawak by Malaysian journalists, academics, and environmentalists. Prominent individuals and political figures became involved. Anthony Brooke, the former Rajah of Sarawak sent a strongly worded letter to the Malaysian High Commissioner in London. In reference to the arrest of Harrison Ngau, he wrote, "No justifiable and acceptable reason has been given for these most undemocratic and repressive measures, which have earned the condemnation of the entire international community." In the USA, the

Congressional Friends of Human Rights, a bipartisan organization of 29 Senators and 133 Members of the House of Representatives sought the release of the Malaysian detainees. Finally, in a widely publicized speech on the global biodiversity crisis delivered at the Royal Botanical Kew Gardens in March of 1990, Charles, Prince of Wales, cited the case of the Penan as an example of cultural genocide.

The impact and significance of this global campaign may be measured directly by the intensity and character of the Malaysian response. The government dispatched high level envoys to Europe, organized conferences, and initiated a media campaign intended to discredit critics. In the wake of his Kew Gardens address, the credibility of Prince Charles was challenged in the press, and the Malaysian government made a strong protest, dispatching yet another mission to London. At the inaugural meeting of the Malaysia-US Private Sector Consultative Group in Kuala Lumpur, Malaysian Prime Minister Datuk Seri Mahathir Mohammed went as far as to suggest that the international campaign had been encouraged by European and North American logging concerns "with a vested interest in protecting their own temperate climate soft timber industry." Malaysian sensitivity was passed into paranoia when it came to the notorious case of Bruno Manser, a Swiss artist who lived for six years among the Penan and whose only legal transgression involved the expiration of his visa. Although blockades, as a tactic, had been used by Dayak peoples for more than a decade, the government held Manser responsible and, according to him, offered a $25,000 reward for his capture. Protected by the Penan, Manser eluded military and police pursuit for three years, and has only recently emerged from the forest to share his version of events with the world.

Despite public statements suggesting the contrary, the governments of Malaysia and Sarawak are clearly on the defensive. In August, 1989, a team from the International Tropical Timber Organization (ITTO), a multinational trade group representing tropical timber producers and consumers in 43 nations, arrived at the invitation of the Sarawak government to investigate logging activities in the state. Their report, expected to vindicate the government's position, instead called for a 30% reduction in the annual cut. Coming from an organization whose primary concern is maintaining the flow of timber to the market, this was a stunning reversal, particularly as the report was published after the Sarawak Forest Department itself had announced that logging rates would be reduced by half during the upcoming decade.

With international pressure mounting, environmentalists are redoubling their efforts to secure a homeland for the Penan, and the protection of the customary rights of all Dayak peoples. The next pressure point is Japan, a nation that depends on Sarawak and Sabah for 90% of its tropical timber imports. Each year between five and six million cubic metres of wood are sent to Japan from Sarawak. The major importers in descending order are Sumitomo Forestry, Marubeni Corporation, Nichimen Corporation, Nissho Iwai Corporation, Ataka Forestry, C. Itoh & Company, Okura & Company, Mitsui & Company, Yuasa Trading Company, Sumisho Lumber Trading Company, Meiwa Trading Company, and Mitsubishi Corporation.

The notion that these and other major Japanese companies are insensitive to criticism and unaffected by the environmental lobby is untrue. In a recent study conducted by the Dentsu Institute for Human Studies, a major Tokyo-based think tank, researchers asked 700 top chief executives how they expected their priorities to change in the near future. Environmental sensitivity ranked third ahead of sales growth, quality assurance, employee benefits, and shareholders. Among those corporations capitalised at more than US$350 million, environmental concern and R&D vied for first place. Although without doubt, Japan lags for behind Europe and North America in terms of environmental awareness, the situation is changing. As Takashi Kosugi, a Diet member and the leading environmentalist of the ruling Liberal Democratic Party, suggests hopefully, "Once Japan decides to do something, it can move very quickly."

The issue, then, hangs in the balance, and a favourable resolution of the conflict — the creation of a Sarawak Biosphere Reserve, the meaningful recognition of Dayak customary rights, and the adoption of sustainable forestry practices — will depend on the actions of each and everyone of us who cares about the fate of the Penan and the other Dayak peoples and their forest homeland. Success will emerge from a variety of strategies. Major environmental organizations will continue to build global awareness of the situation by lobbying corporations, multilateral lending institutions, international development agencies, and the Malaysian governments. They will join in boycotts of tropical hardwoods, participate in informational demonstrations, write letters and circulate petitions. But ultimately, we are all responsible.

Nearly all of the major social changes of the last decades — civil rights, the transformation of the role of women, consumer protection, the rise of environmental awareness itself — began at the grassroots level, catalysed by the dreams and hopes of individuals.

As Randall Hayes, executive director of RAN reminds us, "The fate of the forest is up to each one of us. That's a serious responsibility, but it need not be a burden. To participate wholeheartedly in perhaps the greatest drama of all time, the battle for life on Earth, is cause for celebration. Let your love for the planet express itself as a rock-solid commitment. And then act — starting now!"

Penan Association's Biosphere Reserve Resolution

Whereas the rainforests of Borneo have been the homeland of the Penan people since time immemorial;

Whereas the Penan have been the careful stewards of this forest without damaging it, and we are still dependent upon it for our foods medicines, building materials, water sources and spiritual well being;

Whereas the Penan rainforests are the richest on earth, containing more plant species than any other, unique animal species, and represent a world heritage of unparalleled genetic and pharmaceutical potential;

Whereas logging is destroying the Penan forest faster than any other area of commercial logging in the world and;

Whereas our peoples repeated requests to the governments of Sarawak and Malaysia to spare our forestlands and recognize our rights have fallen on deaf ears, and our peaceful defense of our homeland has met with arrest and imprisonment.

Be it resolved that the Penan Association, acting on behalf of all Sarawak Penan people, calls upon all nations to support the immediate establishment of a Biosphere Reserve to protect Sarawak's last remaining primary forest, its unique wildlife and the Penan's right to their traditional way of life.

Signed this twelfth day of February, 1990

Juwin Lehan, President, Sarawak Penan Association

Witnessed by:

Tu'eu Pejuman (T K Long Iman)   Lukasw Paran   Husein Tu'eu

Directory of Non-government Organizations and Government Officials

Organizations campaigning to protect Sarawak's rainforest and Dayak peoples

Amnesty International
Schweizer Sektion
Postfach 3001
Bern
SWITZERLAND

Australian Conservation
   Foundation
340 Gore Street
Fitzroy, Victoria 3065
AUSTRALIA

Both ENDS
Damrak 28-30
1012 LJ Amsterdam
THE NETHERLANDS

Calgary Rainforest
   Action Group
208 Caniff Place SW
Calgary, Alberta
CANADA T2W 2L8

Community Aid Abroad
National Office
156 George Street
Fritzroy, Victoria 3065
AUSTRALIA

Conservation International
   Foundation
7064 31st. NW
Washington, D.C.
USA 20015

Consumers Association of
   Penang (CAP)
87 Cantonment Road
Penang
MALAYSIA

Cultural Survival (Canada)
Suite 420-1 Nichols Street
Ottawa, Ontario
CANADA K1N 7B7

Earthwatch (Australia)
P.O. Box C360
Clarence Street
Sydney, NSW 2000
AUSTRALIA

Earthwatch (Europe)
Belsyre Court
57 Woodstock Road
Oxford
ENGLAND 0X2 6HU

Earthwatch (USA)
680 Mount Auburn Street
P.O. Box 403
Watertown, Massachusetts
USA 02272

Edmonton Rainforest
   Action Group
51222 RR # 224
Sherwood Park, Alberta
CANADA T8A 1H3

Endangered Peoples Project
P.O. Box 1516,
Station A
Vancouver, British Columbia
CANADA V6C 2P7

Environmental Protection
   Society—Malaysia
5, Jin 20/1
46300 Petaling
Jaya Selangor
MALAYSIA

Environmental Youth Alliance
   (EYA) International
P.O. 29031
1996 West Broadway
Vancouver, British Columbia
CANADA V6J 5C2

Friends of the Earth (FOE)
   —Malaysia
Sahabat Alam Malaysia
(SAM)
43 Salween Road
10050 Penang
MALAYSIA

Friends of the Earth (FOE)
   —New Zealand
P.O. Box 5599
Wellesley Street
Auckland
NEW ZEALAND

Friends of the Earth (FOE)
   —United Kingdom
Tropical Rainforest Action
   Campaign
26-28 Underwood Street
London
ENGLAND N17JQ

Friends of the Earth (FOE)
USA
218 D Street SE
Washington, D.C.
USA 20003

The Gaia Foundation
18 Well Walk
London
ENGLAND NW3 ILD

Greenpeace USA
1436 U. Street NW
Washington, D.C.
USA 7009

International Indian Treaty
   Council
Apartment #1
710 Clayton Street
San Francisco, California
USA 94117

International Work Group for
   Indigenous Affairs
Fiolstraede 10
DK—1171
Copenhagen K
DENMARK

Japan Tropical Forest Action
   Network
(JATAN)
801 Shibuya
Mansion, 7-3-1
Uguisudani-cho
Shibuya-ku, Tokyo
150
JAPAN

Oahu Rainforest Action
   Group
1777 East-West Road
Honolulu, Hawaii
USA 96848

Our Common Ground
2477A Point Grey Road
Vancouver, British Columbia
CANADA V6K 1A1

Penan Association of Sarawak
Long Bangan
Tutoh, Baram
District Sarawak
MALAYSIA

Rainforest Action
Network (RAN)
301 Broadway, Suite A
San Francisco, California
USA 94133

Rainforest Alliance
270 Lafayette Street, Suite 512
New York, New York
USA 10012

Rainforest Foundation
— Australia
P.O. Box 123
Palm Beach, NSW 2108
AUSTRALIA

Rainforest Information Centre
Box 368
Lismore, NSW 2480
AUSTRALIA

Rettetden den
Regenwald e.v.
Hoeseldorfer Weg 17
2000 Hamburg 13
GERMANY

Royal Forest and Bird
Protection Society
P.O. Box 631
Wellington
NEW ZEALAND

Sierra Club of Western Canada
#314-620 View Street
Victoria, British Columbia
CANADA V8W 1J6

SKEPHI
Jalan Tebet Dalam
1G # 35 Jakarta
12810
INDONESIA

Society for Threatened
Peoples — Switzerland
Eigenstrasse 15
CH-8008
Zurich
SWITZERLAND

Survival International (USA)
2121 Decatur Place NW
Washington, D.C.
USA 20008

Survival International
(United Kingdom)
310 Edgeware Road
London
ENGLAND W2 1DY

Sydney Rainforest Action
Group
113 Enmore Road
Enmore 2042
AUSTRALIA

WILD Campaign—
Western Canada Wilderness
Committee (WCWC)
710-340 W. Cordova Street
Vancouver, British Columbia
CANADA V6B 2V3

The Wilderness Society
— Australia
130 Davey Street
Hobart
Tasmania 7000
AUSTRALIA

World Wide Fund for Nature
(WWF)
Avenue du Mont-Blanc
CH 1196
Gland
SWITZERLAND

World Wildlife Fund (WWF)
United Kingdom
Panda House
Weyside Park, Godalming
Surrey
ENGLAND GU7 1XR

**Government officials
directly responsible for
decision-making regarding
forestry practices and the
creation of a Sarawak
Biosphere Reserve**

Prime Minister of Malaysia
YAB Dato' Seri
Dr. Mahathir Bin Muhammad
Prime Minister's Department
Jalan Dato' Onn
50502 Kuala Lumpur
Malaysia

Chief Minister of Sarawak,
and Minister of Resource
Planning (Forestry)
YAB Tan Sri Datuk Patinggi
Abd. Taib Mahmud
Chief Minister's Office
Bangunan Tunku Abd.

Rahman Putra.
Petra Jaya, 93503 Kuching
Sarawak, Malaysia

Minister of Environment and
Tourism
YAB Datuk Amar James
Wong Kim Min
Ministry of Environment and
Tourism,
8th Floor, Bangunan Tunku
Abd. Rahman
Petra Jaya, 93502 Kuching
Sarawak, Malaysia

Chairperson, Sarawak
State Cabinet Committee
on Penan Affairs
YAB Abang Johari bin Tun
Datuk Abang Hj Openg
Minister of Industrial
Development
Ministry of Industrial
Development
13 floor, Wisma Sumber Alam
Jalan Stadium, Petra Jaya
93050 Kuching
Sarawak, Malaysia

Bibliography

Abelson, P.H. 1990. Medicine from plants. *Science* 274(4942): 513.

Anonymous. 1990. Ministry: No one has the right to deprive Penans. *New Straits Times* Feb. 16, 1990.

Aspinall, R. 1989. *Medicinal Consequences of Logging on the Indigenious Peoples of Sarawak, Malaysia.* Western Canada Wilderness Committee.

Bisset, N.G. 1989. Arrow and dart poisons. *Journal of Ethno-pharmacology* 25:1-41.

Broisius, J.P. 1986. River, forest, and mountain: the Penan Gang landscape. *Sarawak Museum Journal* 36(57): 173-184.

Caldecott, J. 1986. *Hunting and Wildlife Management in Sarawak.* World Wildlife Fund (Malaysia), Kuala Lumpur, Malaysia.

Carothers, A. 1990. Defenders of the forest. *Greenpeace* 15(4): 8-12.

Caufield, C. 1984. *In the Rainforest.* Heinemann, London.

Chen, P.C.Y. 1990. *Penans: The Nomads of Sarawak.* Pelanduk Publications, Petaling Jaya, Selangor, Malaysia.

Chin, S.C., Devaraj, J. and Jin, K.K. 1989. *Logging Against the Natives of Sarawak.* The Institute of Social Analysis (INSAN), Petaling Jaya, Selangor, Malaysia.

Colchester, M. 1989. *Pirates, Squatters and Poachers: The Political Ecology of Dispossession of the Native Peoples of Sarawak.* New Series of Survival International Documents #7, London.

Denevan, W.M. and C. Padock. 1988. Swidden-Fallow Agro-forestry in the Peruvian Amazon. *Advances in Economic Botany* 5, New York Botanical Garden, Bronx, New York.

Farnsworth, N.R. 1979. The present and future of pharmacognosy. *American Journal of Pharmacological Education* 43:239-243.

Ibid. 1982. The consequences of plant extinction on the current and future availability of drugs. Paper presented at the Annual Meeting of the A.A.A.S., Washington, D.C. Jan. 3-8, 1982.

Farnsworth, N.R. and R.W. Morris. 1976. Higher plants—the sleeping giants of drug development. *American Journal of Pharmacology* 148(2):46-52.

Grainger, A. 1980. The state of the world's tropical forests. *The Ecologist* 10(1):6-54.

Hanbury-Tenison, R. 1980. *Mulu: The Rainforest.* Weidenfeld and Nicolson, London.

Harrison, T. 1986. *The World Within: A Borneo Story.* Oxford University Press, Singapore.

Hansen, E. 1988. *Stranger in the Forest.* Houghton, Mifflin, Boston.

Hayashi, T. 1990. *The Destruction of the Rainforest and the Natives of Sarawak: The Health of the Penan Tribe.* Report of the Medical Treatment Section, Japan International Volunteer Centre, ms.

Hong, E. 1987. *Natives of Sarawak: Survival in Borneo's Vanishing Forests.* Institut Masyarakat, Penang, Malaysia.

Jermy, A.C. and K.P. Kavanagh (eds.). 1982. Gunung Mulu National Park, Sarawak. Special Issue #2. *Sarawak Museum Journal* New Series 30(51).

Kedit, P.M. 1982. An ecological survey of the Penan. *Sarawak Museum Journal* New Series 30(51):225-279.

MacKinnon, J. and K. MacKinnon. 1986. *Review of the Protected Areas System in the Indo-Malayan Realm.* IUCN.

Myers, N. 1983. *A Wealth of Wild Species.* Westview Press, Boulder, Colorado.

Ibid. 1984. *The Primary Source: Tropical Forests and Our Future.* Norton, New York.

Needham, R. 1953. *The Social Organization of the Penan, a Southeast Asian People.* Unpublished P. Phil. thesis, University of Oxford.

Ibid. 1954. Penan and Punan. *Journal of the Malayan Branch of the Royal Asiatic Society* 27:73-83.

Ibid. 1954. Reference to the dead among the Penan. *Man* 54:10.

Ibid. 1954. The system of teknonyms and death-names of the Penan. *Southwestern Journal of Anthropology* 10:416-431.

Ibid. 1965. Death-names and solidarity in Penan Society. *Anthropologica* 8:58-77.

Nicholson, D.I. 1979. *The Effects of Logging and Treatment on the Mixed Dipterocarp Forests of Southeast Asia.* (FO:MISC/79/8) FAO, Rome.

Ibid. 1965. A review of natural regeneration in the Diptocarp forests of Sabah. *Malayan Forester* 28(1):4-26.

Nicolaisen, J. 1976. The Penan of the Seventh Division of Sarawak: past, present and future. *Sarawak Museum Journal* New Series 24(45):35-61.

Padock, C. 1982. Land use in new and old areas of Iban settlement. *Borneo Research Bulletin* 14(1):3-14.

Payne, J. Francis, C.M. and Philips, K. 1985. *A Field Guide to the Mamnmals of Borneo.* The Sabath Society, Kota Kinabulu, Sabah.

Payne, R. 1986. *The White Rajahs of Sarawak.* Oxford University Press, Singapore.

Pura, R. 1990. The famlies who control Sarawak's forest wealth. *Asian Wall Street Journal* Feb. 7, 1990.

Ritchie, J. 1990. Taib: We're giving due attention to the Penan. *New Straits Time* Feb. 16, 1990.

Sahabat Alam Malaysia. 1986. Native Customary Rights in Sarawak. *Cultural Survival Quarterly* 10(2):19-20.

Ibid. 1987. Sarawak—Orang Ulu fight logging. *Cultural Survival Quarterly* 11(4)20-23.

Ibid 1988. Sarawak Natives' Situation Update (Oct. - Nov. 1988). Interview with Penan Chief. Nov. 14, 1988.

Ibid. 1989. Report of the Sarawak natives defending the forest. Oct. 20, 1989.

Soejarto, D.D. and N.R. Farnsworth. 1989. Tropical rainforests: potential sources of new drugs? *Perspectives in Biology and Medicine* 32(2):244-256.

UNESCO/UNEP/FAO. 1978. *State of Knowledge Report on Tropical Forest Ecosystems.* UNESCO, Paris.

Wilson, E.O. 1984. *Biophilia.* Harvard University Press, Washington, D.C.

Ibid. 1988. *Biodiversity.* National Academy Press, Washington, D.C.

Wong, D.A.J. 1988. The Delemma Penans pose to Sarawak. *New Straits Times.* July 22, 1988.

World Bank. 1978. *Forestry Sector Policy Paper.* Washington, D.C.

World Rainforest Movement and Sahabat Alam Malaysia. 1989. *The Battle for Sarawak's Forests.* Penang, Malaysia.

Zainab bt Tambi. 1982. The nutritional status of children under seven in Sarawak. *Sarawak Gazette* pp.21-29.

Acknowledgements

In thanking the many contributors that have helped make this book a success, we must first and foremost extend our deepest appreciation to Dawat Lupung whose passionate words were the inspiration for this book.

Besides Dawat, there were many other Penan, some mentioned in the book and others who would prefer to remain anonymous, who welcomed us into their homes and shared their experiences. In particular we would like to salute all the wonderful people of Long Penai, Long Bangan, Long Terewan, Long Iman, Batu Bungan, Long Sepatai, Long Akah, Long San, Long Lamu, Long Jekitan, Long Tikan, and Long Bi for their gracious hospitality. To all the Penan and other Dayak peoples *Kaau bakeh ke. Kaau pade ke. Siget kole* You are our friends. You are our brothers. Always.

Our thanks goes to our North American colleagues who assisted in the field; Dr. Ron Aspinall, Duane Foerter, Paul Giacomantonio, John Goddard, Susan Horland, Vicky Husband, Ken Lay, Tim Matheson, Elizabeth May, Josslyn Motha, and John Werner.

Financial support that was needed to make this project a success was generously provided by Rudy Haase and the Friends of Nature, Michael and Anne Talbot Kelly, Sandy Levy, United Nations Association of Canada, WILD, and Bob Weir and the Rex Foundation.

This book has grown directly from the previous efforts of an international network of environmentalists, journalists and academics who have worked for years on behalf of the Penan and other Dayak peoples of Sarawak. In particular we would like to acknowledge Harrison Ngau, Mohd Idris and Chee Yoke Ling of Sahabat Alam (Friends of the Earth) Malaysia (SAM), Randy Hayes and the Rainforest Action Network (RAN) in San Francisco, David Philips and the Congressional Human Rights Foundation in Washington, D.C., Yoichi Kuroda and the Japan Tropical Forest Action Network (JATAN), Yuta Harago of the World Wildlife Fund, Beth Lischeron, Marcus Colchester of the World Rainforest Movement, Roger Graf of the Society for Threatened People in Switzerland, Jennie Dell and Anja Light of the Rainforest Information Centre in Australia, and Jeff Gibbs and the Environmental Youth Alliance (EYA) in Canada.

Because of the format of the book, the authors have chosen not to footnote the material. Pertinent sources, however, are listed in the bibliography. In particular, we would like to draw attention to the resource material provided by Sahabat Alam Malaysia, Friends of the Earth, World Rainforest Movement and Survival International. Marcus Colchester deserves special mention as does Evelyn Hong, whose outstanding book, Natives of Sarawak, is the best single academic source on the contemporary situation of the Dayak peoples.

Actual production of this book was made possible by the special efforts of many people and groups. Financial support came from WILD and the fund raising efforts of Mary Lou Stewart. Lisa Kofod and Shane Kennedy provided technical advice. David Suzuki kindly offered to write the foreword. Adriane Carr provided editorial advice. Tim Matheson, Ken Lay, Jeff Gibbs and Ron Aspinall all donated their photographs. Nola Johnson produced the maps. Bruno Manser reviewed an early version of the text for ethnographic accuracy. Heather Souter and Sarah Khan helped compile and cross reference the list of organizations actively working to save Sarawak's rainforest and the Penan culture. Sharna Searle spent long hours typing and proofreading the manuscript.

In order to meet our publishing deadline and maximize the proceeds that will go towards helping establish the Sarawak Biosphere Reserve, many volunteers undertook the task of collating the pages of this book by hand. To

Claudia Casper, who spent weekends and time after work typesetting this book, and Perry Boeker of Hemlock Printers Ltd., who helped us achieve high quality printing and meet production deadlines, we extend a special thanks.

The authors would like especially to acknowledge three individuals without whose efforts this book would never have been published. Sue Fox Gregory, a co-founder of the WILD Campaign and professional graphic designer, worked without charge for several months on the design and lay-out of this book. In the last frantic weeks, working to an impossible short production schedule, she spent long hours bringing this book to life. Adriane Carr, co-founder of the WILD Campaign, and Paul George, her husband and co-founder of Western Canada Wilderness Committee, both directors of Western Canada Wilderness Committee, backed this project from the beginning. Without their support this book would not lie before you. The time and care that this couple put into this project is but one indication of their selfless dedication to the spirit of wild things.

Because in such a short intense time period so many have helped out in one way or another to make this book become a reality, we know that we have inadvertently left out organizations and people that we should credit and thank. Please accept our apologies. Finally, we want to acknowledge all the individuals and organizations through-out the world who continue to support the Penan and other native peoples in their fight to preserve their wild, rain-forest homelands.

Thom Henley
Wade Davis

September 1990

Published by Western Canada Wilderness Committee (WCWC), 20 Water Street, Vancouver, British Columbia, Canada V6B 1A4. WCWC is a non-profit society dedicated to wilderness preservation through education and research.

Produced by WILD — Wilderness Is the Last Dream — #710-340 West Cordova Street, Vancouver, British Columbia, Canada V6B 2V3. Phone 1-604-669-9453. Fax 1-604-669-9455. WILD is WCWC's international campaign. With a team of staff and volunteers from around the world, WILD is mapping the earth's remaining wilderness areas and is working with other groups to protect and preserve them.

Canadian Cataloguing in Publications Data

Davis, Wade
   Penan : voice for the Borneo rainforest

   Includes bibliographical references.
   ISBN 0-895123-07-0

   1. Penan (Bornean people)—Malaysia—Sarawak.
2. Ethnology—Malaysia—Sarawak. 3. Deforestation—Malaysia—Sarawak 4. Rain forests—Malaysia—Sarawak. 5. Logging—Malaysia—Sarawak. I. Henley, Thom. 1948-   II.
Western Canada Wilderness Committee.   III.
Title.
DS595.2.P44D39 1990   306'.089'99205954
                      C90-091649-4

Printed in British Columbia, Canada, by Hemlock Printers Ltd.
Inside paper stock: glossy—Save-a-Tree—50% recycled (post-consumer waste); bond—Passport Text—50% recycled.